# God is Good

## MARGARET LIU COLLINS

*Oh, give thanks to the LORD, for He is good! For His mercy endures forever. Psalm 136:1 (NKJV)*

REVISED SECOND EDITION

**BOOKSIDE** Press

BookSide Press
877-741-8091
www.booksidepress.com
orders@booksidepress.com

# Testimonials for the author of
# God is Good

*I have known Margaret Liu Collins for many years and knew, in passing, that she had a most vivid journey of faith. Now this wonderful book tells her story and fills in the blanks. It is a personal history, a testimony of her evolving relationship with God and a specific invitation to the reader to go deeper into his/her own unfinished business with God. Reading this book was like reading a letter from someone who was in the apostolic community at the time of Jesus. Margaret crosses timelines, national borders, and expectations in telling this true story.*

**The Rt. Rev. William E. Swing**

**VII Bishop of the Episcopal Diocese of California**

**Founder and President of the United Religions Initiative**

*I resonate with Margaret Liu Collin's memoir as an Asian American immigrant attempting to respond amid life's complexities to the Spirit-filled life made available by Jesus. May those who embark on this journey with her be surprised by how the Holy Spirit can retrieve the pains of our pasts and redeem them for the future God has for us.*

**Amos Yong,**

**Pentecostal theologian and professor at Fuller Seminary**

*Margaret Liu Collins writes from personal experience a "heart-to-heart" testimony to the life of faith and of trust—a hopeful witness for our times. Her strong witness to the life of faith is both fiercely honest and demandingly hopeful. The careful reader will be rewarded by this powerful witness, even when it doesn't correspond to his or her personal experience. Margaret's gift is the celebration of our solidarity of God's love in these challenging times.*

**Alan Jones, PhD, O.B.E. Dean Emeritus of Grace Cathedral, San Francisco, Honorary Canon of the Cathedral of Our Lady of Chartres**

*Margaret Liu Collins is a spirit-led person who puts Jesus first in her life. She is acquainted with the Holy Spirit and has a great desire to see people come to know the Lord as she knows Him. She shares her spiritual life and walk with people boldly and openly. It reminds me of the biblical story of the two men encountering the risen Christ as they walked along the road to Emmaus. They later exclaimed, "How our hearts burned within us." This is what happens when the Holy Spirit comes, and Margaret, having had such an experience, shares that in this book and encourages others to find life eternal through Jesus, and then to be guided and directed by the Holy Spirit in every area of life. This is the one to whom she gives credit to her success and blessing in life – —to the one who has shown her the way.*

**Peggy Cole, Peggy Cole Ministries, International Evangelist**

*This book has been one of the most important Christian experiences that I have ever had. I just love it. Mrs. Collins is so intelligent, yet so simple in her faith...that anyone from 10 to 100 years old can read this book, and completely understand it. She talks throughout about her personal relationship with the Holy Spirit; how He teaches her, leads her and protects her. But, you soon come to see that her life, although fully blessed today in every way, was not always so. She, unlike so many other ministers, who only reveal the ups and victory in their lives, shares transparently how sometimes she has missed it. This is the key to her life, to face and admit that no-one's life is perfect but if we keep hearing from God in prayer and faith, He will lead us into victory.*

**Terry Haggins, Pastor of Victory International Church**

*I've the honor of working with Margaret and learned from her both professionally and spiritually, when she served as a board of director at ComplianceEase, a RegTech company I co-founded in 2001. Born in the turbulent 1940s in China, Margaret accepted Christ in early age and faithfully seeking His face even when life throws her curve ball. In her book, Margaret describes vividly how she grew up and thrived in a traditional family of gender bias and negligence. How a young and divorced single parent struggled with making ends meet by only leaning to God. How a devastating mother of strong faith in prayers moved God's hands, and He delivered her son from a near death car accident. By listening and obeying Him, Margaret made God her General Partner in the real estate business that He has blessed her financially.*

*Margaret's story is merely manifesting how Holy Spirit could transform and guide our life only if we trust and obey Him.*

**John I. Vong, Executive Chairman, ComplianceEase, a SitusAMC company**

*This book is Margaret Liu Collins' living testimony of God's goodness, an excellent example of how amidst life's great turmoil, heartache, and unexpected twists and turns, obedience to the Lord, loving the Lord with all of one's heart, and loving others as one's self are the keys to untold blessings and true peace. In this book Margaret shows great truths, nuggets, and practical examples that help the reader to know God, to grow in their faith, and develop a wonderful relationship with the Lord. I have learned so much from her as an example. God is good! All the time! Amen.*

**Charmaine Shen, Ambassador for God, Fellow sister in theLord.**

*Margaret witnesses to all of us how to live a life leading by God and filled with the Holy Spirit. She put her life experiences in words even though she had to relive the hardship she went through. But with God's loving nudging which prompted her to finish writing this heart-felt work of arts during the pandemic. Margaret taught me "How to be in an Ever-Present, Continuous Conversation and Communion with God". Through hearing the voice of God, she changed her career from a teacher to a real-estate broker. She seeks God's will for every major decision and she acts on it immediately. Her obedience to God's guidance set a valuable example for us all to follow. Thank you, Margaret for writing this book that allowing all who reads the book to be inspired and blessed.*

**Lily Lee**

*Some people are put on earth to do good in this lifetime. Margaret Liu Collins is one of them. Her journeys through tough marriage, injury of her son Samuel, and other hurdles in life have made her a better person, willing to help others and contribute to the community via doing the Lord's work. She has been rewarded for this in abundance.*

*By reading Margaret's book "God is Good," I have learned several important messages:*

* Forgive, but not forget.

* Wealth itself is worthless unless you use it for God's Glory.

* The three faces of Stewardship: multiply, save, and give away without hoarding.

*I would recommend this book to inspire others.*

**R. Pang**

*Margaret Liu Collins doesn't preach. She shares her Christian faith with the reader and uses her own experiences to illuminate how it enriches her life.*

**RPP**

*I enjoyed reading about Margaret's life and how she responded to adversity. I thought I knew Margaret but this book explains a lot about how she conducts her life. When I think about good people - and I mean pure goodness - Margaret comes to mind. Perhaps, it was God who made her good or, perhaps, it was through her own hard-earned work and wisdom. She thinks positively and treats everyone with goodness. It is excruciating for her to utter a negative word about anything or anyone. Although she's weathered horrible hardships, she simply worked harder to escape the trap of being/staying a victim. Margaret is an inspiration to me.*

**Amazon Customer**

*Margaret gives you a front row seat of her intimate walk with her Heavenly Father, sharing her prayers with the Lord as well as sharing not just the highlights but also the lowest points in her life. With the spiritual gift of teaching, Margaret is able to help believers deeply understand and apply the Word in prayer and in daily life. She gives practical ways to hear the voice of God, to partner with the Holy Spirit, and to minister the gospel in love to your community!*

**Jasmine**

*A profound telling of how following God's guidance resulted in transformation of a miserable life to success, abundance and happiness.*

**Edward C.**

*Practical, insightful steps to a deep walk with God, from a very successful business woman. Rarely do we get to peek into the private and spiritual life of a real estate and business magnate. She shares how God led her into a life of success through trust and faith, in a way that leaves you with a practical blueprint for the abundant life.*

**Kristy C.**

*Amazing life stories. Praise the Lord!*

**John Vong**

*Knowing Margaret personally, after reading her book, I now understand fully her wonderful relationship with God. A great and inspiring read.*

**Amazon Customer**

*Margaret witnesses to all of us how to live a life leading by God and filled with the Holy Spirit. She put her life experiences in words even though she had to relive the hardship she went through. But with God's loving nudging which prompted her to finish writing this heart-felt work of arts during the pandemic. Margaret taught me "How to be in an Ever-Present, Continuous Conversation and Communion with God". Through hearing the voice of God, she changed her career from a teacher to a real-estate broker. She seeks God's will for every major decisions and she acts on it immediately. Her obedience to God's guidance set a valuable example for us all to follow. Thank you, Margaret for writing this book that allowing all who reads the book to be inspired and blessed!*

**Amazon Customer**

> \* *If you are in a bad or abusive relationship, lookingfor a way to get out*

> \* *If you are at the end of your road, can't find analternative*

> \* *If you are looking for supernatural helps and comforts*

> \* *If you want to find a formula for success in life*

> \* *If you want to have instance heavenly assistance inyour decision makings*

* *If you want to have miraculous guidance form above*

* *If you have any doubt about God's existence*

*Then God is Good book is for you. Through these pages, Margaret Liu Collins shared her invaluable life experiences that we can learn from. She paid the horrible prices, but at the end, her conclusion is still "God is Good" because undoubtedly, God is Really Good! This book will help you to find out for yourself!*

**Chi Pan**

*A fascinating and beautiful book written by Margaret Liu Collins on how to walk with God and step by step instruction on how to receive what God always wanted for humanity: abundance in spirit, friendships, finances and advice on things from food to marriage. Many of us are inthralled in fights, resentment, revenge, and small turmoils that plug our communication path and we forget that there is someone who is ready to help as long as we are ready to receive and listen.*

*Exceptionally written with many life examples that give us glimpse into Margaret's life and her surroundings. Highly recommend for anyone who is seeking to discover what life with God can be.*

**Maya Valentine**

*GOD IS GOOD leads reader to follow Margaret Liu Collins step by step Daring FAITH, inspired by the Holy Spirit in Healing and Speaking in Tongues.*

**Marina Tsang**

*I just finished this book and got on amazon to purchase a copy for my sister. Would highly recommend it! This book is an easy read and will encourage you no matter what season of life you find yourself in. It's written with a great deal of humility and the helpful take aways are so practical. As the book does such a great job illustrating-God is good!*

**Amazon Customer**

*A powerful story of how a "good girl who was raised to be seen and not heard" discovered the power and authority available to her as a daughter of the King of Kings. She discovered her gifting and passions through a loving relationship with her Creator, cultivated in her earthly relationships as a daughter, wife, dedicated mother, then successful businesswoman, and philanthropist.*

**Em Essie**

*This book is a gift to me and I enjoyed reading it. Margaret provides a strong testimony on experiencing God's greatest love, presence, help & Grace to her as she put her trust in God and walk in faith. Praise the Lord!*

**Amazon Customer**

*I was recently gifted this inspiring book, it gives hope with God's guidance. I am not a religious person, but reading through it really made me wanting to know God better. I particularly enjoyed reading Margaret's personal stories with her intimate experiences with God. (All is with God's Grace and miracle)*

**Tiffany Chang**

*GOD IS SO GOOD. Must Read!!*

**JLH**

*This is such an inspirational biography of the writer; the messages she conveyed ascertain the Love, Grace and Mercy one can receive as a family member in His kingdom. Her Daring Faith in Christ is something that encourages me to build upon. Thank you for writing this amazing book!!*

**Gorretti Lui**

*An unselfish sharing of intimate events of her personal life. Very moving, inspiring, and motivating. A must read for all ingood times and in challenging periods. Greater than life itself! Thank you so much for sharing.*

**Zon**

*Amazing testimonies and breakthroughs with God's help and grace that sustains. This is an inspirational book that gives you hope and encouragement. Thanks for sharing your story.*

**Kathy O.**

*Indeed, Margaret speaks from her heart, and her life story is candid, uplifting and inspirational......yes, all things are possible with God!*

**Ira Hillyer**

*I couldn't put it down. Ii read it cover to cover in an evening and the next morning. It was given to me as a gift. Highly inspirational.*

**Elena C. Beyers**

*An inspirational story about Margaret's triumphant journey by having faith and submission to God.*

**EL.**

*Good testimony and very inpirational.*

**Faber Tan**

*Margaret's personal life history is so inspiring!*

**Cameron Emmott resdMD**

*I was inspired and comforted while reading this compelling story. I have always been fascinated by people who become successful in spite of early circumstances that would not inspire success. How does a woman raised in a traditional Chinese family where females are considered "second class", who then finds herself married to a mean and belittling husband, break free and become successful? Not just successful, but extraordinarily successful in business and a powerful philanthropist supporting others and making major contributions to her community. Some of the answers will surprise you. This book was fascinating on multiple levels. Highly recommended!!*

**Nettsky**

*This enlightening book is one to be read thoughtfully.*

*The author, Margaret, generously shares her conversations with God as He guides her through many of the storms and ordeals of her life.*

*She provides practical encouragement on how we too can talk to God; God who is available to guide us, to support us, to comfort us.*

*With its well chosen bible verses the book illustrates the nearness, the availability of God and how we can rely on Him to answer even the smallest prayer.*

*God is available to help us.*

**VJM**

*Margaret's wisdom and personality shine throughout this account of her personal journey with a kind, communicative and forgiving God. Her book contains many wonderful lessons that will lead us to productive , well intentioned lives guided by the voice of God.*

**Rosalyn Meyer**

*Margaret has written an inspiring and emotionally moving account of how relying on and trusting God has transformed her life and can do the same for you. Margaret lived through tumultuous times. She was born in a time of war, escaped from the cultural revolution in China, grew up in a family where girls were treated as less than boys, married an abusive man, raised her children alone, and had a tragic accident befall her child. Through all these events, Margaret shares how God can work in you with the power of the Holy Spirit to get you through the tough times and, more importantly, to experience the blessings that God wants you to have as you walk with Him. The joy and love of the Lord that Margaret has comes through every page. Margaret wrote this book so that you to can have this joy and love. I treasure this book and know you will also.*

**Kindle Customer**

*"God is Good" is a highly readable, accessible testimony to a surprisingly modern relationship with God. Using down to earth examples and analogies like real estate investment, eating wontons, GPS, and Arnold Palmer drinks, Collins offers a user friendly guide to hearing and accepting God in your everyday life.*

**Amazon Customer**

*Well written and great author.*

**Denise**

*"God is Good" is a very touching, inspiring, and powerful book of belief. Margaret Liu Collins tells her personal stories of her long journey guided by God throughout her life. As a Chinese American, she describes in detail how God helps her with her family, her marriage and her children, and how God assists her in making hard decisions in her non-native country. The book is in three parts. Part One tells about how God offers her freedom from her unfortunate relationships; Part Two details how to recognize God's will and God's voice; and Part Three demonstrates the power of the Holy Spirit. Step by step, God leads her to get rid of darkness, to strengthen her self-confidence, and to overcome the obstacles. Through her personal experiences, she firmly believes that God is always there for her, and ready to give her advice. The book is a powerful witness of her walk along with God who becomes her constant companion. In addition, there is a special feature throughout the book. The*

*comic strips accompany each chapter, which makes the reading moreenjoyable.*

## Mengxiong Liu

*This book was a gift given to me by a very special person - I will treasure it.*

*Margaret Liu Collins has written a very moving book telling of the almost unbelievable hardships she and her family have faced. Her abiding faith in God has guided her through these trails and tribulations, allowing her to become a very successful business woman, and true defender of people in need from all walks of life. Truly inspirational.*

## GKM

*Author's personal relationship with God throughout her life's journey is inspirational and meaningful to all. Collins' own challenges and successes in life validate the omnipresence of God through his spirit of understanding, love and guidance. Reader will appreciate Collins' resiliency and gratitude as well as her commitment to philanthropy.*

*"God Is Good" is a good read for everyone's heart and soul.*

## Victoria F

*I really enjoyed reading this book! This book is filled with amazing testimonies the author has experienced.*

*The true goodness of our Father IN HEAVEN and how He longs to give us all His best for us. Author has taught us howto completely surrender to God starting by the smallest matter( her dumpling story ^^ ).*

*You will not regret reading this book and I highly recommend!! It is a true testimony of a Godly woman and how*

*God is using her for His purpose. Praise the Lord for He istruly good!!*

## Amber F.

*Margaret Liu Collins' Powerful, personal testimony in always placing 100% faith and trust in God, has led her to an exceptional life of great success, achievements, and philanthropy. In this book, Collins shows God exemplifies grace, mercy and abundance, which He wants for all of us. God's love is immutable, and he will never forsake us. God is Good is a witness to the readers that no matter what circumstances or hardship we face, we must accept God in our hearts, involve Him in every single aspect of our lives, and our Heavenly Father will Always lead us to the right path.*

*This book has inspired me greatly!*

**Sabrina Iwate**

*Excellent testimony that everyone should read!*

**Stephen Wu**

*Ms Collins book was a very inspirational read. I throughly enjoyed how she explained in very practical examples from her own life - some dramatic and devastating and some more quotidian - how her faith is woven into her essential fabric and how it guides her as her compass. Besides those lessons, I was impressed by her life story so it was a biography and life guide in one book! I enjoyed her perspective on how God views material wealth and the responsibilities that brings to those who are fortunate. I enthusiastically recommend God is Good!*

**Marie D. Welch**

*As Pastor Tim Keller says, "God is not passively good, He is actively good." Sis. Margaret's book "God Is Good" not onlyreveals the goodness of God but also gives us practical guidelines as to how everyone can experience the goodness ofthe Lord in their lives. Her testimony is so inspiring and encouraging and gives hope to the reader that the Lord who has done wonders in the life of Margaret, can and will do great things even in their lives.*

**Pastor Ezra Thomas,**

**Senior Pastor, Church Of The Living God, Pune**

# Note about Scriptures and Abbreviations

Many scriptures are quoted throughout this book.

Each scripture has been selected from the specific translation of the Bible that most clearly communicates the idea being conveyed. The translated forms and their abbreviations include:

Amplified Bible (AMP)

American Standard Version (ASV)

Contemporary English Version (CEV)

English Standard Version (ESV)

Good News Translation (GNT)

King James Version (KJV)

The Message (MSG)

New King James Version (NKJV)

New International Version (NIV)

New Living Translation (NLT)

# CONTENTS

Testimonials for the author of God is Good.................................iii

Note about Scriptures and Abbreviations .............................xvi

Why This Story? An Introduction.........................................2

Part 1: God Offers Freedom from Toxic Relationships ......................6

    Chapter 1: Separating Human Purpose from God's

        Plan for His Children.....................................9

    Chapter 2: Finding God's True Voice at a Crisis Point.............20

    Chapter 3: How God Provides for Us—All of Us

        —Not Just a Little Bit, But with Abundance.........24

Part 2: How to Recognize God's Will and God's Voice

    (And Distinguish it From My Own).........................30

    Chapter 4: The Importance of Having a Pure Heart

        When We Seek God's Will .....................................32

    Chapter 5: How to Discern Our Own Desires and the Distractions

        of the World in Order to Hear God's Voice ............70

    Chapter 6: How to be in An Ever-Present, Continuous

        Conversation and Communion with God...............78

Part 3: The Power of The Holy Spirit .................................86

    Chapter 7: Who is The Holy Spirit, and What are

        the Powers That the Holy Spirit Offers Us? ...........91

Chapter 8: How Do We Stay in the Constant

Presence of God Through the Holy Spirit? .......... 112

Chapter 9: How the Holy Spirit is Present in Our

Financial Affairs ................................................. 199

My Cherished Desire .......................................................... 231

From the Mouth of Babes—Samuel Liu, My Son ............................. 236

Resources and Inspirations ............................................. 238

Acknowledgments........................................................... 242

About the Author............................................................ 245

However, as it is written: "What no eye has seen, what no ear has heard, and what no human mind has conceived" — the things God has prepared for those who love him — these are the things God has revealed to us by his Spirit.
— 1 Corinthians 2:9–10 NIV

# Why This Story? An Introduction

Early in my Christian walk, I was fearful of God. I did not want to come to God because I was afraid that I might have done something wrong and that He would punish me. I was not sure that God is always good. I had the idea that God is in heaven looking down on me, getting ready to punish me for my wrong deeds.

In my walking with the Lord, reflecting back on my relationship with God from the beginning and through many decades, I came to a deeper understanding and realization that God loves me and is good all the time. God's intentions since creation have always been out of love and for our good because God is good.

*In the beginning God created the heaven and the earth. Then God looked over all He had made, and He saw that it was very good! Genesis 1:1 and 31a (NLT)*

For many years, when I would tell friends about the events of my life, they'd tell me that I should write a memoir because God has favored me and blessed me. I resisted. I'm not a writer and don't pretend to be, and a memoir seems to be more about the person telling it than any story that I'd want to tell.

You see, my life and my choices are not the focus of this story, as it would be if this were a traditional memoir. The focus of my story is not my early life in China, the customs in my family that made me, a daughter, into a second-class citizen, my immigration to the United States, or my first marriage, which was an abusive one. It is not the story of my experience of starting with barely enough to care for my children, to having a life of financial abundance and success today. Yes, all of those things are my experience, and I will share some of that, but that is not THE story I'm trying to tell. Though I'm a mother who loves my children, this is not a story of motherhood. As a newly single mother with two small children, I had nothing but the need to adequately provide for my children and that drive led me to great financial success, a true success story that many would find interesting. But that is only part of the story that I am called to tell.

I am a daughter, a mother, a wife, and a woman who has been blessed by God with great financial success after leaving an abusive marriage and doubly blessed with a second husband who is kind, loving, and supportive beyond measure. All of that is true, but this story only includes me; it is not *about* me. And that is why I so resisted writing my story for so long.

As the years have passed, and as I've entered the autumn of my life, I've felt a gentle nudge—a long series of nudges, really—to share what is really my story, or truly, what is the real story *under, around, and throughout* my story.

This is not a story of my own triumphs and pains. I'll share these events, but not to talk about me and my life. Rather, I'll share my life's events as examples to illustrate how each triumph is a direct result of the intimate relationship I have with God, with Jesus Christ, and with the Holy Spirit as the unified force in my life. I came to understand God's role in my life in degrees, and over time, from the age of thirteen until today, which finds me on the cusp of my ninth decade, and I'll hope to continue to grow in His grace and understanding for the remainder of my time here on earth.

I'm sharing the story of God's lessons to me, ones that I've learned through experiences both challenging and triumphant. So many people, including me in my early Christian walk, have a view of God as a judgmental, punishing God. But the story I'll share here is that God wants us all to have joy, peace, safety, security, and abundance. When we seek and welcome God's revelation, instruction, inspiration, opportunity, and guidance, all things are possible.

This story is a set of moments, snapshots, if you will, where I'll share events of my life and the way in which God taught me, delivered me, restored me, revived me, supported me, protected me, nurtured me, and guided me. Even at my advanced age, I am continuing to learn about God's immeasurable love for all of His children and His capacity to help them create lives of happiness and abundance of every kind.

Even the existence of this book—a book which I at first resisted writing—is evidence that I continue to strive to hear God's calling, to share His goodness, and to encourage those who struggle to find comfort in God's loving embrace. It is the story, as the title implies, of God's immense and immutable goodness and love. It was God, through His Holy Spirit, who kept nudging me to write it.

And so… I have.

God insisted I write this book. Not once. Not twice. But many times, He laid it upon my heart that I was to write it. I am no Hemingway. I am no celebrity. I am not a person of great contribution to society like Leonardo DaVinci or Winston Churchill. English is my second language, and I have never taken a course in writing but for English 1a and 1b in college. But now, after completing this book and receiving feedback from others, I can see the purity, wisdom, and beauty of God. It is He that is the true writer of this story. God can use the most humble and weak vessel to pour out his love and holy message to the world. I am honored that He used me as such a vessel.

How abundant are the good things that you have stored up for those who fear you, that you bestow in the sight of all, on those who take refuge in you. — PSALM 31:19 NIV

# Part 1

## God Offers Freedom from Toxic Relationships

*And I will give you treasures hidden in the darkness—secret riches. I will do this so you may know that I am the Lord, the God of Israel, the one who calls you by name. Isaiah 45:3 (NLT)*

*The Lord hears his people when they call to him for help. He rescues them from all their troubles. The Lord is close to the brokenhearted; He rescues those whose spirits are crushed. Psalms 34:17-18 (NLT)*

Everything in my life, and background, taught me the value of commitment, loyalty, responsibility, and integrity. This was most especially true of my view toward marriage. My parents, the Chinese traditional values and culture with which they raised me, and my Christian faith combined together into a strong and unwavering message: *Marriage is an exclusive, unbending, lifelong commitment. Divorce is not an option. This is how I entered marriage at age twenty-two.*

Though the memories of my first marriage are dark ones, the lesson God taught me during and after that time is the pure white light of His divine love and grace. It was through the challenges of my marriage that I came to understand God's immutable love, mercy, grace, and true desire for His children. When I was going through darkness, I was unaware that God had hidden treasures and riches for me. Because of that difficult period, I learned to treasure what many people take for granted.

Though I will tell you of some dark moments in my early married life, mine is not a "woe is me" story. In fact, it is quite the opposite. It was in this time of darkness that God's true light shone through, and I learned to hear His deeply loving voice. As you read the story that follows here, I invite you to consider the value of learning to listen to God's truest voice as separate from our temporal, human judgment. I ask you to be open to thinking of God's love for us differently than you might have been taught to think of it—different than I once thought of God's love. It is by learning to listen to the true voice of God—as did Noah, Abraham, Jacob, Joseph, Moses, Samuel, David, Esther, Ruth, and Mary (the mother of Jesus), as well as the Apostles in the New Testament long before me—that I learned that every one of His children is invited to reap the harvest of love, abundance, good health, peace, and joy that He offers to each and every one of us. ***Suffering and ill health are not God's plan for any of us.***

In Part 1 of this book, I'll address three aspects of what God has taught me through my experience before, during, and after an abusive marriage. These were the experiences where I learned about how we are to live in His holy grace. Though I am mere human, flawed and still learning, I have learned to welcome God's lessons for my life, and I write now to share this with others.

**The three lessons I will address in Part 1 are as follows:**

- Chapter 1: Separating Human Purpose from God's Plan for His Children

- Chapter 2: Finding God's True Voice at a Crisis Point

- Chapter 3: How God provides for us—ALL of us—not just a little bit, but with abundance

I have come into the world as a light, so that no one whosoever believes in me should stay in darkness.
—JOHN 12:46 NIV

# Chapter 1

## Separating Human Purpose from God's Plan for His Children

I was born in Chongqing, China, in the early mid-twentieth century. It was a tumultuous time in China—my birth country was then an occupied nation during the second Sino-Japanese War. On my second day of life on Earth, my mother was carried out of the hospital on a bamboo stretcher as patients were being evacuated to a bomb shelter; as this happened, she held me in her arms. Despite the horror and massacres around me, I was, even from the beginning, secured in the love of my parents. My father worked for the Central Trust of China and was sent to the United States to attend NYU for postgraduate study, where my family stayed from 1944 to 1946. Once back in China, my parents would escape to Hong Kong in 1948. Later, when I was seventeen, I left home to attend the University of California at Berkeley, where I majored in chemistry.

I was the first-born of my parents, who were admirable people. For the first eight years, I was the apple of my parents' eyes, happy, healthy, and cared for within the family. I was born average in many ways that may seem a contradiction to the life of abundance and accomplishment that I now lead—all of which is attributable to God's influence in my life. I was taught modesty and respect, and followed closely the Chinese traditions of obedience and honoring my parents, as well as avoiding any behavior that might shame them or cause my family to lose face in their community. Quite simply put, I was a very good girl in the ways that my Chinese parents expected me to be—I did not question them or any of the rules and customs by which I was taught to abide.

When I was eight, my brother was born. As was the longstanding tradition in Chinese culture at that time (and unfortunately, one that continues today in much of the culture), a boy is a much-favored child over a daughter and the heir-apparent. The warm light of my parents' adoration for me faded, and instead, the glow of it shone on my brother. He became their everything; I became invisible. My brother, simply by virtue of his gender, could do no wrong and was lavished with all of the attention (and far more) that I once received from my parents. Though I remained obedient and did all that I could to honor and please my parents, it was my brother who received their praise. Once happy in their light, I began to feel I was of no value. I can see now how this image of myself later allowed me to think that I must tolerate treatment that nobody should tolerate and that God does not intend for His children to endure.

As far as my attitude toward my brother was concerned, I was very happy and proud to be his big sister and enjoyed taking care of him. I have not stopped loving him from the first time I set eyes on him the day he was born at French Hospital, Kowloon, Hong Kong. I harbor no resentment, jealousy, or bitterness today, though I must admit that I had such moments earlier in my life. As I understand intrinsically, my parents were upholding 4,000 years of Chinese culture and tradition by favoring a son over a daughter. Despite this, I am thankful that God gave me a brother to love and care for.

My learning of the values of obedience, modesty, and honoring my parents and ancestors continued when I attended St. Stephen's Girls' College, an Anglican high school in Hong Kong. By the time I was twenty-one, my junior year at UC Berkeley, my father was pressuring me to marry. I was well educated. I came from a good family. I was obedient, cheerful, and quiet. These things made me a desirable bride, and I had several suitors from whom to select a husband.

My selection—I'll call him Ex throughout this story as there is no purpose in my sharing his name—seemed perfect. His father was an elder in the local church that we attended, and his sister was my roommate at Cal. When he wooed me, I was impressed with his brilliant intelligence and his devotion to God. He was a fountain of compliments, praising me for my qualities, lavishing attention upon me. To say that he was romantic would be a gross understatement. He was positively gallant, generous, and adoring. He placed me on that proverbial pedestal, seeing me as perfect. I felt adored. I was an innocent then, not only in the ways of the flesh but also naïve of heart. So I did not know to look deeper—past his romantic gestures and his glowing adoration—to know the man beneath the facade. And truly, he was also very convincing.

I would learn in the most painful way that there is a vast difference between being adored and being loved, respected, and honored.

This marriage began as most do, under an umbrella of idealism and romance, promises of affection, and with the intention of unending commitment—*until death do us part.* These were vows I made with sincerity, fully intending to honor them for life.

Shortly after our wedding, Ex became distant. I thought it was because of the pressure of getting his Ph.D. in Physics. Initially, it began with criticisms in which he would blame and demean me. This was a painful change from the romantic, wooing suitor I'd married. Of course, I wanted to please my new husband, so I went to the Lord. "Is there a lesson for me?" I prayed. "Do I need to adjust my attitude or behavior?" I repented for my shortcomings, thinking that I was, as Ex said, not a *good enough housewife.*

So at first, I attributed Ex's negative commentary to my shortcomings. I was raised to study hard and excel in academic studies, but with little expectation or training in what were then the traditional American household duties of a wife. Because I was sincere about my inquiry to God and about my dedication to making my marriage work, I set about to learn how to be a better wife. I approached it as I had in researching my studies. Soon I learned to purchase the best produce, to mop and wax the linoleum floors until they shone, to clean the oven and copper-bottomed pans until they gleamed. I learned to shampoo carpets and to properly and efficiently iron Ex's shirts. I worked diligently to improve all of my home-making skills.

Meanwhile, Ex seemed dedicated to sabotaging my efforts. He left his clothing, newspapers, and all other belongings in constant trails of messes around the house. He tended to be a hoarder, refusing to part with even the most useless of items. When I say useless, I'm not talking about someone who holds onto too many books or tools. He retained used motor oil from when he changed it in the car, ten years' worth of old newspapers stacked everywhere, used razor blades, and hundreds of other items that most anyone would consider garbage. Truly nothing was discarded. I viewed his messy trail as my task to clean, thinking it was there simply because he didn't have time to deal with it, though later, I attributed his clutter to his qualities as a hoarder.

I set about to master the other household skills to please my husband as well. My father, like so many, told me that the secret to a man's heart was through his stomach. I studied cookbooks, trading recipes, and learning cooking skills from friends and a chef from Peking Restaurant. After a few years, I became a skilled enough cook to host an entire banquet meal to entertain Ex's friends and business associates.

Despite all of my progress in learning to cook and clean, Ex's criticisms mounted. Nothing was adequate. He complained about the cost of everything, and that is when I realized that money was a major issue for him.

While being frugal and careful with money can be an admirable quality, and one that I continue to value, Ex took it to extremes. Every penny he had wore a bruise from his pinching of it. He was not frugal; he was miserly, bitter, and angry about any expenditure. Despite his successful position, he was upset over every expense. To prove that I could be a good wife, I again began to study. I learned to sew our children's clothing, made slipcovers for furniture, draperies, and bedspreads. Back then, one could economize a great deal by making, rather than buying such things. Again, thinking my efforts to economize would please my husband, I was stunned when the opposite was true.

If I questioned him or displeased him in any way—which was utterly unavoidable, given the absurdity of his expectations—I punctured his illusion that I was "perfect." By Ex's measure, he deserved perfection, and if I did not reflect the perfect image he expected, I was worthless. He was perfect; I was a failure. The bloom of his adoration withered and died, leaving me with no pedestal and with no love to replace it.

Looking back now, I realize that Ex's charms during our courtship were a manipulation, the tools he needed to gain me as a conquest. It was a competition against the other suitors—which I believe made me more attractive to him—so he used his best skills to stand out and to win the contest. As soon as we were married, Ex was no longer in pursuit. The conquest had been made, and the charms were no longer necessary. That is when his true self emerged.

He would insult and attempt to humiliate me at every turn. He ridiculed me for whatever he saw as the smallest infractions in meeting his absurd and mercurial expectations. Every day he made it his mission to tear me down and to make me feel small and worthless. He wanted to control my every move and had ridiculous standards and expectations. Though I'd try in every way to please him, this proved impossible. Nothing I did was right. Nothing could ever be right. He was menacing and threatening, occasionally physically—a cowardly act of a man toward his wife and children.

Despite the presence of abuse, I continued to try to be the dutiful and obedient wife that my parents, my Chinese culture, and my later adopted Christian values. I constantly prayed for God to help me, for him to soften Ex's heart.

Eventually, I became unhappy, and I became despondent. Life was painful. I felt trapped by my bad mistake of selecting this man, of being fooled by his charms.

It was hard enough to endure the abuse alone, but once our two children arrived, it became unbearable. I was terrified by the idea of divorce and afraid of the stigma that it might cause for my children. Divorce was much less common in those days, and I feared the children would suffer if Ex and I parted. I grew isolated, withdrawn from friends and community, and without a church community.

The only saving grace in my marriage was that Ex loved work above most everything else and worked long hours, and sometimes his work required him to be away from us for weeks and months at a time. This was a mixed blessing, as when he traveled, he left few resources for children and me. In addition to his miserly ways, Ex saw any expenditure needed by the children and me as unnecessary.

Given that I'd discovered how important money was to him and that I was so determined to make my marriage work, I decided to try even harder. *Bring in income!* Ah, yes. I thought I'd figured it out, found the missing piece to my marital happiness puzzle.

I prayed for a part-time job to subsidize our income and to ease Ex's resentments for every nickel that was spent on our home or our children. Samuel, my second child after his sister, Magdalene, was under a year old. God answered my prayers with a substitute teaching job in the nearby school system. This was my way to honor my husband, to offer some ease to his worries about money, obsessive and irrational as they might have been. I was willing to step up and share his burden as breadwinner.

Logic might tell you that this would please Ex, that my stepping up to contribute financially would cause some praise. But no, it was not to be. Instead, he mocked my earnings, telling me, "You have no talent for making money."

My boss in the school district admired my work and

offered me a full-time job if I got a teaching certificate in New York, where we lived at the time. I attended night school at New York State University, Stonybrook, Long Island, working diligently toward the goal of earning a bigger paycheck to please Ex. No sooner had I received my certification than Ex announced that we would move to New Jersey. He had a better job offer.

This meant that I had to get yet another teaching certification in yet another state. But I did it. And after we lived temporarily in a small rental home in Parsippany, New Jersey, God was gracious in providing me with a teaching job in a nearby town with good schools for the children.

Ex's stingy ways continued. He determined that other than a few pieces of living room furniture and a piano, we needed no other furniture when we moved. I shopped at garage sales to furnish the children's rooms, and my parents sent a Chinese rosewood dining room set to us from Hong Kong.

While my children were small, we lived in Long Island and later in New Jersey. Ex would work but did little else in the way of being husband or father. When he was at home, instead of acting like a loving father and husband, he controlled us. He allowed my children and me only one to two meals per day. We were allowed to flush the toilet in our home only one time per day. And, even during frigid Long Island winters, we were not allowed to turn on the heat. This was not because we were poor by any means. Ex had a good job and excelled in his field. This was not about money; this was all about his sovereignty over us. He was the king, and we were his meager and unworthy subjects.

People may wonder how I could be so foolish as to follow these unreasonable rules. But you must remember that I was taught, by family, by culture, and by tradition, to be obedient to my husband.

Within a few years, Ex got restless again. He got a job offer in California, and off he went, while the children and I remained in New Jersey. After a year, Ex returned and announced that we were moving to Cupertino, California.

We saw little of Ex in Cupertino. He came home only long enough for a quick dinner and a few hours of sleep while the family was totally ignored. That's when his verbal devaluation became even worse.

He was argumentative and complaining every moment he was at home. Our home atmosphere was one of turmoil and strife. Joy, harmony, love, and mutual caring were mere fantasies that had no reality in our home. Ex was either hot—blaming, accusing, criticizing, or picking fights over nothing—or he was cold—ignoring the mere existence of the children and me, our family.

My Christian faith has been a constant in my life, even during those years of abuse. So, I persevered. I assumed that God was trying to perfect my way of expressing His love. I thought it was God's will for me to learn to love those closest to me, even the ones who did not love me. This was my human understanding of God's love at that time. I used the Bible to try to understand and as a source of guidance.

*Love is patient and kind. Love is not jealous or boastful or proud or rude. It does not demand its own way. It is not irritable and it keeps no record of being wronged. IT does not rejoice about injustice but rejoices whenever the truth wins out. Love never gives up, never loses faith, is always hopeful, and endures through every circumstance. I Corinthians 13:4-17 (NIV)*

I would only later learn the true meaning of the love described in Corinthians and that it did not mean that one should endure abuse as an act of love.

Back in the San Francisco Bay Area, I had the support of a strong Christian community. The members of my church prayed for my family and me. And I prayed, too. My sincerest desire was that my marriage was going to work for my children, for God, and for my parents in Hong Kong.

Though my ex-husband continued to conduct his

reign of terror, the idea of divorce seemed impossible. Divorce was prohibited by my culture, by my faith, and by my family.

I had a sense that perhaps I did not pray well enough to hear God's perfect will for me. The Bible became an even more important companion and the words of Jesus a comfort.

*Father, if you are willing, please take this cup of suffering away from me. Yet I want your will to be done, not mine. Luke 22:42 (NIV)*

Despite it all, eventually, I had to tell my parents of the abuse. My mother came from Hong Kong and tried to mediate, as Ex was usually on his best behavior in front of her. He put on a very different face for her than the one that my children and I knew. But his true colors were revealed, even to her one day when Ex announced to her that he'd never wanted children. These were her grandchildren he was talking about! This gave my mother a glimpse into who Ex really was.

I was born during some of the most tumultuous years in China. There were three wars going on simultaneously: the Sino-Japanese War, the Civil War between KMT and the communists, and World War II. It was a time filled with fear, deprivation, and danger. Having endured hardship early on in life, I grew up able to tolerate a lot. But the abuse in my marriage was tearing me down to nothing. I felt broken, powerless, and trapped. I did not know if I could sustain a marriage under such conditions. The members of my church would pray for me, but they stuck to their idea that ending my marriage was against the will of God. I was in a jail that had no bars, and my children shared my cell. I prayed and prayed, but the abuse continued. It seemed that I got no answer.

What I know now, looking back, is that I was trapped in the rules of my culture and the erroneous teachings of my church, both of which disallowed divorce under any circumstances. Those in my church at the time saw divorce as against God's will, without exception. These were the *human* interpretations of God's will. In so many of our churches, we are taught that suffering is an indication of our piety, a requirement in our relationship with God. In the immature stage of my faith at that time, I believed this too. Today I understand that it is legitimate to end a marriage that is abusive, which mine certainly was.

*"For I know the plans I have for you," says the Lord. "They are plans for good and not for disaster, to give you a future and a hope." Jeremiah 29:11*

But God intervened and revealed to me His truest desire for the life He had planned for me. The verse above from Jeremiah really speaks to me. I was most surely headed for disaster. But God's plans for me were better—far better. God wants us to have a life that is above and beyond, overflowing with abundance.

That is the next part of the story.

Here I am! I stand at the door and knock. If anyone hears my voice and opens the door, I will come in and eat with that person, and they with me. — REVELATION 3:20 NIV

# Chapter 2

## *Finding God's True Voice at a Crisis Point*

While much of Ex's abuse of me, and later my children, was verbal, psychological torture—unreasonably controlling, constant belittling, insults, denial of our basic needs—he eventually became physically abusive as well. Although there are many incidents I can describe, there is no reason to itemize each horrible event. This is not a book of complaints.

Instead, I will tell you about the one event that pushed me into crisis—the one that pushed me into God's loving arms.

My daughter Magdalene was eleven. My son Samuel was seven. I cannot now recall the details of what set Ex off on that particular day. It could have been something as small as a toy placed on the coffee table or a facial expression that Ex decided was insubordinate. Truly though, it was likely nothing but his own mood of that moment. All I recall of that incident is seeing my young son's body flying across the room, propelled by Ex's hand, causing little Sam to hit the wall with a giant thud. It took my breath away to see my child taking the abuse of a grown man, his innocent little body tossed as though it was a piece of garbage.

That day, my prayers took on a new voice. I was upset with God. But I was also honest and deeply sincere in my plea to Him. "God," I prayed. "If you are a loving God, how can you allow a young boy, my son, to suffer like this? I do not mind you trying to teach me lessons through suffering. But it is not right for my son to suffer abuse at such a young age. How can you stand by and do nothing?

You are a God of love. Are you going to do *something*? My church community has prayed for me day and night for ten years. Hasn't that been enough?"

I had never before dared to talk to God in such a tone, but I was truly desperate these verses were brought to my mind:

*I poured out my heart, baring my soul to God, my God. Daniel 9:3b (MSG)*

*If you look for me wholeheartedly, you will find me. I will be found by you, says the Lord. Jeremiah 29:13 (NLT)*

I knew that God must understand my agony. After all, He watched His own Son suffer and die unjustly at the hands of those who were too blind to understand what He was offering to them. I finally said to God, "If an abusive husband is my cross to bear in this life, I will do so if it is your will. But I am merely a human mother. I cannot watch my children suffer at such a young age. They are innocent. You cannot ask this of me." You see, I still then believed that God would have me suffer. I later learned that God doesn't want any of His children to suffer.

In less than a week, my prayer was answered in a most unexpected way. Quite out of the blue—or so it might seem to some—Ex served me with divorce papers. He had refused to consider this before, adamant that divorce was out of the question and that all of the problems in our marriage were my fault. My prayers had been answered, but in a way, I'd never have predicted. On top of gaining freedom from an abusive husband and father, I was spared the act of going against the teachings of my church and the expectations of my family, causing them shame. It was more than I could ever have hoped for.

I had been seeking God's help. But I'd been asking for it through the limitations of my human understanding and the judgments that I'd learned through man's interpretation of His will. I'd been taught that divorce was unthinkable under any circumstances. But with God's intervention—and I know that it would be ONLY through Divine intervention that Ex's heart could have been so changed—that He gave me His most important message. The message is this: God is Good. He wants to deliver us from bondage and suffering.

The depth of this truth is among the most powerful of God's lessons for all of His children, and one that changed the entire course of my life. It is also a key message to understand in order to enter into an authentic, loving relationship with God. After all, who could possibly love and trust a God that wanted our suffering? Knowing that He wants deliverance from our abuse and our happiness, wants our safety and wants us to live in abundance changes the very nature of our prayers—our conversation with God.

The lesson for me that came from this time in my life:

God is more than happy and willing to be involved in our lives, to assist us, and to help us to be happy and well. But we cannot be complacent and passive. We must invite His help. It was when my prayers were honest and sincere, my conversation with God authentic and from my heart, that His answer was given.

It was after my divorce that I learned a second crucial lesson about God's will for our lives. That is the lesson that created the life that I have lived ever since, and I'll share that in the next chapter.

**MISTY** A **Joyful 'toon** by Mike Waters

Why, you do not even know what will happen tomorrow. What is your life? You are a mist that appears for a little while and then vanishes. — JAMES 4:14 NIV

# Chapter 3

## How God Provides for Us— All of Us—Not Just a Little Bit, But with Abundance

It will likely surprise no one that Ex was no better as a former husband than he was as a husband, though his absence did spare my children and me the constancy of his abuse. I felt free for the first time in many years, and I was grateful to God for providing the answer to my prayers—that was the key to my freedom. Ex did no better at providing for me or for his children after the marriage than he did during the marriage. When he left, he took most of the furnishings in our home and emptied every cent of cash out of all of our shared accounts.

By then, we lived in Cupertino, in the South Bay of San Francisco's Bay Area. With Ex's departure, my means were limited, and even then, expenses were high in this area. During the period of our separation, Ex was forced by the courts to pay me temporary support and mortgage and utilities for a time. The permanent alimony and child support was one hundred dollars per month per child and one hundred dollars for me. And yet, he did not pay even this meager sum. My lawyer had to write him letters to insist on even this. He fought everything and dragged his heels. Every time he did so, it meant that I had to come up with another $5000 to pay another retainer fee to the attorney to get Ex to fulfill even the most basic of obligations. A $5000 fee may not sound like a lot, but in 1978 and on a limited income, with two small children, this seemed impossible. For only $300 a month, even if I had the money, it wouldn't make sense to spend so much pursuing it. So, I let it go unpaid. It was clear that I needed to provide for my children and myself and that Ex had no intention of helping.

I knew I could not adequately support my children and myself with my teaching salary alone, which was, at that time, $35,000 per year. I was most concerned about their future. I calculated a rough budget, determining that I needed to obtain approximately one hundred thousand dollars for my two children's future college education. That seemed impossible to me at the time.

So, I prayed. And by then, I'd grown more comfortable talking with God in my everyday life. I had experienced that He was a good God, not the vengeful God I'd heard about. I'd once talked with Him only for "the big stuff." But I had learned that He was there for me in the everyday, about matters big and small.

*Trust in the Lord with all your heart, and lean not on your own understanding, in all your ways acknowledge Him and He shall direct your path. Do not be wise in your own eyes. Proverbs 3:5-7a (KJV)*

At that time, I was learning that there were two ways of looking at solutions to problems: God's way and my way. I prayed and was learning to trust God's way of answering and in His time, not my own. God did not answer my prayers overnight. And I had learned that the delay in God's reply to our prayers is not because he's busy playing Mahjong with the angels. No. God is never too busy for us. Rather, He waited, not for His needs, but for my heart to surrender to Him and to learn to align my thinking with God's thinking.

I had things to learn. I had to learn to put ego aside and to seek His will with a pure heart. I had to learn faith and trust in God. I asked for the ability to provide for my children and to take care of myself. In His reply, God's voice was clear and unwavering after several weeks of my prayers. With crystal clarity, He told me to go into real estate.

*What?* This confused me. Real estate? I'd never even

thought of such a thing. I had been a science teacher and knew nothing of real estate and sales. I had no credentials, no experience, and had never had any aim to enter this field. But because He had answered my prayer, prompting Ex to initiate a divorce, I continued to talk with God. You see, being in conversation with God means that He is always available and always willing to welcome your heart. You can voice your doubts, your objections, and your confusion. You can even express your anger as I had done in the darkest moments of my first marriage. He wants us to be our authentic selves in our conversations with Him. I expressed my confusion.

To that, God replied, "Have I ever made a mistake?"

I decided to accept this simple truth. God does not make mistakes. He always has the best and good intentions for me. He was calling me to act on His word.

*I stepped out in faith, and this was the best step ever.*

Immediately, He gave me the wisdom to enroll in three different community colleges simultaneously, taking every real estate course required in California. Money was limited, and I had small children, so I had to do this with great haste. I took the classes, passed my realtor's test, and obtained my real estate license in three months. I credit this, not to any exceptional brilliance on my part, as I mentioned, I was born average in many ways. I attribute this to my surrender to God and honoring Him with my hard work and dedication.

We could not live as we had, and the house we had shared with Ex was filled with bad memories. Using my half of the home's equity that I obtained during the divorce process, I purchased another, more modest home in the same community to keep my children in the same school district and their lives as stable as I was able. Though my children were now safe from Ex's daily ill-treatment, they had been traumatized from the time they were born. It was important that I provide a home where they could heal and grow. I needed that as well.

With my basic needs a bit more secure, I was able to

turn my attention to my new profession. Though I had a real estate license and basic knowledge, I remained unsure of how to proceed. God had provided the direction, and I had followed His will with my commitment and dedication. But what next?

I took a job in a real estate office under a broker. While I tried to appear professional, I wore only the modest clothing that my limited budget allowed. The broker said that I needed to improve my appearance and dress in a way that communicated professionalism. At first, I balked at this idea. I had worked hard and wanted my boss and clients to judge me for my hard work and dedication, not for the package I would be wrapped in. But God's guidance arrived through the voice of my own mother. I told her about my broker's instructions but stated that in heaven, it would be the content of my character that would be of value and not the package that contains it. But my mother told me that I wasn't in heaven yet, and that on Earth, 95 percent of people look at the package, not the content.

With limited funds, I went to the Salvation Army thrift store and scouted out the most professional clothing I could find. When I returned to work, I was stunned to find that people instantly perceived me as smarter, more capable, and more successful.

This may seem like a small moment, but it was a major turning point in my life. It is a lesson that was true in that business context, but it has also been true in my life, testifying about God's goodness and abundance. The package is what people see; the content of our testimony is what they may be more willing to hear if they find our presentation desirable.

An engineer from Southern California was relocating to the South Bay. I was able to find a home for him in the city of Saratoga. It was that big first sale that instantly made me the top salesperson in the company. It was the opening of a door that would open many doors for my future in real estate. God had not brought me the one hundred thousand dollars I'd asked for; He'd provided a means to many times that much. God was not just a *little bit* good, He was *very* good. But I was clear; this was money to be used to not only provide for my children and to allow us to live in abundance. It was money to also be used to glorify God. I would need to be a good steward of what He'd given to us.

I was fortunate enough to be interviewed by CBN for the 700 Club on this matter. The following is the link to this short video of that interview: https://www1.cbn.com/ divorced-single-mom-conquers-finances

Soon, it appeared that I had the Midas touch, though I know it was not my touch at all, but God's. It was His goodness and favor.

Word traveled in the wealthy community of Chinese people in Hong Kong, and soon, I had listings and facilitated sales of many millions of dollars. Within five years, I had moved from buying my clothing at the Salvation Army to becoming a millionaire, with exactly the abundance that God had told me I would achieve.

This is not simply a "rags to riches" story. Tha would be the human story that we see in so many films. No, this is a story of God's goodness, His immutable love, and His desire for each of us to live in abundance, to be delivered from suffering, and to accept His divine influence in our lives. This is not the story of just me, of how God helped me toward a life of freedom from suffering, from financial worry, and from the limitations of the human interpretation of God's will as a series of restrictive rules and laws. Rather, mine is the story of how God can be a presence and the source of God's grace in everyone's life if only we invite Him. Through the empowerment of the Holy Spirit, we can all, each and every one of us, move from the "natural," seen world and walk in the "supernatural," unseen world where miracles happen, and God's grace, abundance, and joy reside.

Above all else, guard your heart, for it is the wellspring of life.
— PROVERBS 4:23 NIV

# Part 2

## How to Recognize God's Will and God's Voice (And Distinguish it From My Own)

**Introduction to Part 2**

If I have learned nothing else from my long journey in this life, it is this: *To be truly happy is to live in alignment with God's will and to be in ever-present communion with Him.*

To live in harmony with our Heavenly Father, to walk with his Son Jesus Christ, and to be empowered by the Holy Spirit brings a life of peace, health, joy, and blessings to all. But how does one discern what God's will is? How do we recognize His voice, telling it apart from our own desires and from the influences and messages that we are bombarded with every day?

This earthly life is filled with distraction—those people, activities, and forces that mimic God's voice or distract from it—keeping us not only from hearing the voice of God but rendering us unable to recognize it when we do, unable to tell His voice from our own will.

When we succumb to following the voice of our own desires, are distracted by the ways of the world, or are seduced into accepting the world's definition of a "good life," we find that we are living separate from God's Word, and from the blessing that is available through His holy grace. This is a life far less fulfilling than the one that God offers to each of us.

God is always present, always right there for each and every one of us without exception. When we learn to recognize and listen to God's voice, nothing can separate us from His divine love.

As you read the following chapters, I invite you to recall those times when you have felt as though you are truly walking with God, when you felt that God was speaking to you. What did that feel like? What were the results? I'd also invite you to recall those times when you either disregarded His voice or couldn't discern it from your own or from the messages that this earthly or secular world offers as a way to live. What resulted from that?

God speaks to us if we ask. He is omniscient, omnipresent, and omnipotent—always available to us. Learning to recognize and heed His voice is our pathway to a life of peace, joy, health, and heavenly blessings.

The three lessons we'll explore in Part 2 are as follows:

Chapter 4: The Importance of Having a Pure Heart When We Seek God's Will

Chapter 5: How to Discern Our Own Desires and the Distractions of the World in Order to Hear God's Voice

Chapter 6: How to be in An Ever-Present, Continuous Conversation and Communion with God

# Chapter 4

## The Importance of Having a Pure Heart When We Seek God's Will

*Seek ye first the kingdom of heaven and His righteousness and all these things will be added unto you. Matthew 6:33 (KJV)*

It became clear to me in my walk with God that my deepest desire is to lead a life acceptable to Him, a life that glorifies Him. This felt challenging as I went through my first marriage, as I described in Part 1. And though a part of me trusted God, I am but human, and I would sometimes doubt. Fear about my ability to provide for my children would creep in. It is hard to hear God when our minds are cluttered with our needs and with the needs of our children, our elderly parents, and for some of us, the care of our siblings.

But I learned that God is always available, and that His voice is our clearest guide during challenging times, as well as during times of abundance. Most of our time and energy goes into managing the details and worries of the "natural" kingdom, the earthly existence that we lead. This is a world filled with anxiety, fear, expectations, and worldly temptations. But God wants us to be focused upon His "heavenly kingdom," the world of love, abundance, mercy, peace, joy, grace, and intimate and ongoing communion with our Heavenly Father. If we are willing to love God with a pure heart, He reveals His purpose to us, and this is equally true whether we are struggling to make ends meet or if we live in comfortable abundance.

**God Answers All Prayers, But…**

Before I delve too far into the idea of seeking God's will and of learning to hear His voice, it is important that I share a concept that I once found difficult to understand, but gives me great comfort today: *God hears and answers every prayer; it's true.*

*The Lord says, "I was ready to respond, but no one asked for help. I was ready to be found, but no one was looking for me." I said, "Here I am, here I am!" to a nation that did not call on my name. Isaiah 65:1 (NLT)*

*You don't have because you don't ask. James 4:2b (CEB)*

It is important to know that His answer to our prayers is not always yes. In fact, God has three answers to our prayers: yes, no, and wait. Many people have this notion of God as though He is a genie, granting the whims of whoever rubs the lantern and makes wishes. But God is not a magic genie. He is not the granter of wishes. He is our Heavenly Father, and each of us is a child whom He loves.

*The Lord is good to those who wait for Him, to the soul who seeks Him. Lamentations 3:25 (NKJV)*

Every parent knows that he or she will receive many requests from their children. We love our children, and we want them to be happy. So it seems that it would be easy to make them happy every time they ask for something by saying yes to everything and doing so instantly. But good parents know that sometimes the requests of our children are not reasonable, not healthy, or not in their best interests or the interests of others. Sometimes we say no because we know that our children have a lesson to learn. Say that our child has not completed her homework, and she begs us to let her stay home from school, saying that she doesn't feel well. We know that she is avoiding the consequences of her actions. We know that staying home under false pretenses will only serve to reinforce her procrastinating her schoolwork. We also know that going to school, getting marked down on a grade, and facing the teacher's disappointment may just be the proper way for her to learn the lesson she needs. So, we say no.

When we act in our children's best interests and say no, children do not turn to us and say, "Thank you, Mommy. I know you only said no to me because you love me and know what's best for me." Rather, children (sometimes even adult children) get upset with a "no" response from their parents to their requests. They want what they want, and they want it now. Their desires may be unsafe or unhealthy for them, and we, as their parents, know better and must say no. Our children's requests may be too costly or too troubling to others. They may be asking for something that may go against our values. Weak parents indulge these requests. Strong, wise, loving parents are willing to endure their children's temporary disappointments for the greater long-term good.

Sometimes the timing is the issue. Our children ask us for something that may be okay to give them, but the timing is wrong. Or perhaps we don't know if we can say yes because we're waiting on other information to surface so that we can answer rightly. We need to see how our finances work out, or we need to ask for someone else's input before we can respond. As much as children do not like to hear no, they also do not like to hear "wait." They get impatient. Small ones throw tantrums. Older children sometimes argue with our choice or commit acts of defiance.

As parents, we have lived longer than our children and have experienced more than they have. We know more about the consequences of our actions. If we've learned lessons from our own choices (good and bad), we bring wisdom that our children may not have into the decision-making process. We have both experience and foresight as well as authority over our children.

We, children of God, treat our Heavenly Father in much the same way as children treat their earthly parents. We think that if we pray for something and God's answer is anything but immediate and affirmative that He is not answering our prayers at all. But our Heavenly Father—just as we should be as human parents—has our best interests at heart. He is all-knowing of the past, the present, as well as the future. He can foresee the outcome of the decisions we make. So sometimes He says no or wait instead of our desired yes.

God, with His benefit of omniscience and omnipresence, can see far ahead and knows that what we want may be good, may change, or simply that the timing is not quite right. He knows what circumstances will be revealed over time or what events may occur to change what we want or even when what we request could be harmful to us in the long run.

It is also important to know that despite His omnipotence, God has also endowed us with free will. Sometimes when God speaks to us, even so clearly that we cannot doubt that it is His voice guiding us, we exert our own will. We believe we know better, or simply, like our earthly children, we want what we want. At these times, we override God's direction with our own will. Even when we disregard God's voice, He remains with us—omnipresent—available always to accept our prayers.

God is not a genie, granting our every wish. He instead is more like a loving parent. He listens to every prayer and answers it—yes, no, or wait. That being said:

*Elijah was a person just like us. When he earnestly prayed that it wouldn't rain, no rain fell for three and a half years. He prayed again, God sent rain, and the earth produced its fruit. James 5:17-18 (CEB)*

*God, Wonton, and Me: Learning to Hear and Obey His Will So faith comes from hearing, that is, hearing the Good News about Christ. Romans 10:17 (NLT)*

For years from the time I accepted Jesus as my Savior at the age of thirteen, I was a dutiful religious Christian. By this I mean, I went to church every Sunday, rain or shine. I went to youth meetings and joined the choir. In college, I participated in morning prayers with a group of students every day. Sometimes I was in the spirit, feeling connected with God, but most of the time, I was in my mind and my emotion, worried about my grades, and being homesick. As much praying as I did, I remained in my mind, worrying and feeling anxious. I was not in my spirit walking in faith, peace, and joy. I did not yet have an intimate relationship with God. I then viewed God as someone "way out there" in outer space, someone who had a lot of rules and laws that I should obey like I obeyed my parents.

Though I prayed, I was not sure He heard me and would answer my prayers. Nor did I ever hear from Him. I read Andrew Murray's book Abide in Christ and understood the theory of its premise, that Christ is the vine and that we are the branches and that the Holy Spirit flows from the vine and to each branch. As I said, I understood this in theory, but I did not then understand how to flow in the life of the vine.

Then one day, I read a verse in the Bible that turned the light on for me.

*Jesus replied, "You must love the Lord your God with all your heart, all your soul and all your mind and all your strength." This is the first and the greatest commandment. And second equally important "Love your neighbor as yourself." Matthew 22:37-39 (NLT)*

Now, this may be a verse that is familiar to many of us. But there are times when even a familiar verse takes on a transcendent meaning, especially when we read or listen to it with an open heart.

I was deeply touched by this verse because I knew that God loves me; that was at the root of my Christian faith. But this verse became alive in me and I suddenly knew how to interpret these words and apply them to my everyday life in practical ways. It put me in mind of how we are to love God in return. God loved me so much that He gave His only begotten son, Jesus, to die for me. The least I can do is to respond by loving Him with my all heart, soul, mind, and strength.

But how do we, on Earth, show God in heaven our love for Him? This was my question. With the verse from Matthew that I've cited above, God showed me the very simple and practical way I could demonstrate my love of Him.

God wants us to do our best in our every activity, personal and professional. I needed to be conscientious, whether it is a task I love or one that I don't like so much. We who are devoted to God must be conscientious in all of our endeavors. We must execute tasks to our best abilities, always—even those necessary tasks we find disdainful. If I show love to the people around me, and in whatever project I embark upon, this is how I demonstrate my love to God.

Jesus did not want to die on the cross for us. He asked His Father to "remove this cup" from Him. But Jesus demonstrated His love of the Father by ultimately obeying and doing that which he did not want to do.

Sometimes we are asked to do what is difficult. I'm comfortable in the world of math and finances. I'm comfortable trading stocks and managing accounts. But I know in my heart that God wanted me to write this book. And I'll tell you, dear reader, that I did not want to. I don't feel that I write well. I don't like doing it as English is my second language. I do not express myself well in English. I resisted. I tried to abandon the project many times. I procrastinated. But ultimately, I heard God's voice, and I obeyed. If Jesus could die on our behalf, my obedience to God on such a small thing as writing when I do not want to and do not feel qualified is a small sacrifice to demonstrate my devotion.

*Blessed are those who hear the word of God and obey it.*
*Luke 11:28 (KJV)*

So, my prayers changed. I prayed with my heart open, with my mind focused on God, and with my soul dedicated to Him. With that, I heard God's calling. I consecrated and dedicated myself to God "to love Him" as He loved me. I was willing to surrender all that I was, past, present, and future, to the Lord.

Back to the discovery of that verse. When I read it, I realized that I needed to surrender to God and to serve Him with my every effort. So, I did. Immediately following this prayer of surrender and seeking, I was having lunch. My favorite food was then (and still is) wonton. In those days, I often ate twenty-three wontons at one sitting. So, I began to eat the delicious, yummy wontons. Then when I was about to eat the fourteenth wonton, I heard the Lord's small voice, saying, "Stop eating Margaret. No more. That is enough."

I was surprised that the Lord talked to me about something so small as eating wonton. But I knew in every bit of me that this was God speaking to me.

Prayer is a two-way conversation, you see. So, I responded to the Lord with my confusion. "When I consecrated myself to you, it is for the big things in life such as my future on the macro scale, not such mundane stuff for you to micromanage me on the number of wontons I eat."

His response to me was precise; He brought to mind this verse:

*If you are faithful in little things, you will be faithful in large ones. But if you are dishonest in little things, you won't be honest with greater responsibilities. Luke 16:10 (NLT)*

I was annoyed. I felt as though I did not need someone else bossing me around on every small thing, to be micro-managed by anybody. But I had a desire to hear God's voice and to be in an intimate relationship with Him. Reluctantly, I submitted and surrendered my will to Him, acknowledging His headship over me. I obeyed and stopped over-consuming my wonton, finding that I could still be satisfied without being overindulgent.

Now looking back on this small step of obedience, I see that it has really been the biggest blessing to me for the rest of my life because not only did I never again overate and thus never struggled with my weight, but I also found that I could be in conversation with God on every matter, big and small. He was there with me, offering guidance on something as small as eating wonton, and later, He would be available on huge life matters, instructing me on how to prosper and take care of my children after my divorce. I overcame the lust of eating—a lust of flesh—by being obedient to the prompting of the Holy Spirit. I also demonstrated that I was willing to obey. This may seem a small thing. But learning to be obedient to God and to hear His voice on small matters is as important as on big matters.

From that moment on, I was more sensitive to the prompting of the Holy Spirit, and I was able to be receptive to God's voice on matters big and small. This was a major turning point in my walk with God. This was my surrender, my becoming truly consecrated unto God. This was the beginning of my ability to hear the small voice of God in my everyday life and the start of my close walk with Him.

The constant presence of God in my life, with His holy voice as my guide, is the single biggest blessing to me. The Lord is available to my prayers and responds with His voice. Though, as humans, we are flawed and can be inconsistent, this is not true of God. He is ever-present, always available to speak to us, if only we listen to Him.

### Maturing in Our Walk… and Our TALK… with God

Have you ever been driving, trying to tune into a radio station you'd like to hear, but static or a weak signal keep you from hearing the broadcast? For a time, that's how it felt for me when I tried to hear God's voice—either static or no signal.

Today in my walk with the Lord, hearing God's voice is as natural and easy as hearing the voice of my loving husband, or listening to the voice of a friend on the phone—or turning on the radio in my car and listening to good music. But it has not always been that way. I used to struggle to hear God in my daily life. Prayer, and particularly the *listening* part of prayer, like anything else, is a skill at which we can grow more proficient with time. We learn different techniques for conducting our conversation with God from our unlimited spirits rather than from our finite minds.

Life is hectic and stressful. When we are distracted, emotionally distraught, we often struggle to tune in to God's voice. He is always there; His voice is a constant transmission for us to find. But the static of our daily lives can make it hard to hear.

Praying and singing God's praise quiets the static and tunes us into the frequency of God's voice, clear, strong, unwavering. And God's voice doesn't go silent, even when we drive through a tunnel.

I've found worship music especially helpful in bypassing my own distractions and opening the channel to hear God's voice. Music and gleeful praise elevate our spirits, bypass our distractions, and help us enter the presence of God. I invite you to find your way to praise and worship and can tell you that it will lift your spirit while God is glorified and that it will help you to hear His voice with strength and clarity.

For fun, I'll share a few of my favorite worship songs to help you on your way. I find these to be a quick and easy way to enter into God's presence. You can find them for free on YouTube:

**Artist: Dan Moen**

*Thank You, Lord*:

https://youtu.be/K44trVhtZX4

*Lord, I Offer You My Life*:

https://youtu.be/37u6IBRDgm8

*House of Hero's Worship, Come Holy Spirit*:

https://youtu.be/QyAypM0hsm4

*House of Hero's Worship, Hallelujah*:

https://youtu.be/lcta2ObQ6Ng

**Artist: Terry MacAlmon**

*Hallelujah, Hallelujah*:

https://youtu.be/dueyN1VqQn0

*Come Holy Spirit*:

https://youtu.be/JrqCB11qbVw

Bear with each other and forgive one another if any of you has a grievance against someone. Forgive as the Lord forgave you.
— COLOSSIANS 3:13 NIV

## The Obstacle of "Unforgiveness": My Biggest Challenge of Faith

Being in communication with God also requires that we clear the pathway for communication. If we think of conversing with God as talking on a two-way radio, He is always sending out the signal to talk to us, and He is always ready to receive our communication as well. God's side of the communication is always a clear signal. But on our end, on the receiving end of the communication, we often have static or distraction that keeps us from "hearing" God's messages, and sometimes that "noise" blocks us from talking to God in the most unencumbered way. When we are active in sin, this scrambles communication. And when we are encumbered with resentment and bitterness, it blocks the clear channel to talking with God as well.

Perhaps the biggest challenge to my faith—as well as God's most vivid demonstration that He heard my prayers—occurred about a year after my divorce from Ex. It was also a time when I was released from bitterness, anger, and resentment.

The year following my divorce was full of so much conflict, resentment, and anger. Ex was ordered to pay $300 per month, but he rarely, if ever, paid it. I was struggling financially. I was in a state of worry. I was angry and disgusted at Ex for the abuse that had taken place during the marriage and his lack of taking responsibility for his children afterward, though he was financially well able to have been of more help to his children.

It was at about that time that my son, Samuel, suffered a terrible accident. While crossing the road after school, a drunk driver without insurance hit Samuel, tossing his small body ten feet into the air. His head landed on the concrete middle partition of a two-way divide road causing terrible head injuries and internal bleeding that resulted in a coma. After fifteen days in his coma, the internist and neurologist gave us little hope for his recovery and prepared us for the fact that he could either die, remain comatose, or could live, but with severe physical and cognitive impairment. I was warned that should he come out of the coma one day, he could remain in a vegetative state for the remainder of his life. This is every loving parent's worst nightmare.

The members of my church fellowship held Samuel up in prayer and provided great support to me during that time. A sister in the church asked me one day to read and meditate on the following passages carefully and every day:

*Then Jesus said to the disciples, "Have faith in God. I tell you the truth, you can say to this mountain, 'May you be lifted up and thrown into the sea,' and it will happen. But you must really believe it will happen and have no doubt in your heart. I tell you, you can pray for anything, and if you believe that you've received it, it will be yours." Mark 11:22-24 (NLT)*

That first verse told me of the vastness of what was possible through prayer. The next one that my church sister offered let me know that my faith did not have to be perfect in order for God to answer it.

*"You don't have enough faith," Jesus told them. "I tell you the truth, if you had faith even as small as a mustard seed, you could say to this mountain, 'Move from here to there, and it would move.' Nothing would be impossible." Matthew 17:20 (NLT)*

These verses gave me comfort. They truly did. At that point, my faith was indeed as small as a mustard seed. I faithfully read them and prayed every day. One day, as I read beyond these specific verses, the matter of prayer and how it relates to "unforgiveness" struck me.

As I continued to pray, the Holy Spirit revealed to me that I was holding on to resentment and anger. When we are living in a state of unforgiveness, we are ensnared in a tangle of bitterness and resentment. I came upon this verse that I took to heart:

*But when you are praying, first forgive anyone you are holding a grudge against, so that your Father in heaven will forgive your sins, too. But if you refuse to forgive, your Father in heaven will not forgive your sins. Mark 11: 25-26 (NLT)*

My desperation to have Samuel recover was so enormous that I wanted nothing to get in the way of God hearing my prayers. I wanted no sin in me to be an obstacle to my talking to God or for His answer to my prayers.

At that time, my faith had grown, and the Holy Spirit usually gave me great peace, but of course, I'm a mere human mother, so it was natural to be worried. In addition to the natural worry over my son, I found that bitterness and resentment about Ex were a big presence. In addition to shirking his financial responsibilities, Ex also shirked his fatherly responsibilities when it came to Samuel after his accident.

While I was a near-constant presence in Sam's hospital room, Ex came to the hospital only once. Samuel was in a coma for thirty days; Ex visited for exactly one hour. When he did finally visit, Ex brought along a woman that was half his age. The whole time they were there, not once did either of them inquire about Sam's condition or about how they might be of any comfort or assistance. During their brief visit, the young woman constantly sat on Ex's lap as if she were his daughter.

Watching all of this unsettled me deeply. I wished for people to be next to me, helping me out, supporting me during this trial about my son. I was not jealous of the younger woman. I was frustrated to be so alone at this time as my son faced a matter of life and death. Holy anger rose up in me. Anger, bitterness, resentment, and all of the grudges I was holding in my heart rose up, rekindled by his abhorrent behavior and, no doubt, my worry for my son. Memories of every criticism, every bit of neglect and humiliation he had caused during our marriage hovered around me. Memories of his mistreatment of our children loomed large in my mind. That one and only visit he made to the hospital rattled me to my core.

I had been in prayer for my son many times a day following his accident. I actually had peace that passes understanding because God told me that He is with Sam and with me. But when I went to my knees in prayer on the day Ex had visited the hospital, I did not have peace. I was in turmoil. As I meditated on those now-familiar Bible passages, God's word comforted me and reassured me that the mountain of my son's injuries would be removed. But that's when the Lord said to me:

Margaret, you have so much turmoil. So much anger, bitterness, and resentment. You are holding on to grudges and disgust for Ex. You are to get over your past experience and move on. You must get rid of this because it hinders your prayer to the throne room. These negative emotions open the door and give a foothold to the demonic forces and spirits. Look at how I forgive you of all of your misgivings, past, present, and future. You are to do the same with Ex. It is futile to remember the terrible past. Forgive and move on. The best is yet to come for you. Let go of this horrible past so you can enjoy the bright future I have planned for you.

As a younger woman, I'd been tangled with the spirits of fear, cowardice, and timidity. God had given me boldness, confidence, and strength. The Holy Spirit conveyed to me that by letting go of the past, I have the power and authority in the name of Jesus to command that bitterness, resentment, and anger should also be banished. I exercised my "believer's authority" and commanded those negative emotions to leave me in the mighty name of Jesus.

This was my decision to let go, and with God's help, I did. It was not easy in the beginning. I would go for a time without the anger and resentment, and then it would creep back in and bother me at night or when I was alone or stressed. But I persisted in my prayers and, in Jesus' name, I *insisted* that those negative emotions leave me.

I was fighting for my son's life. And every day, I

was in this spiritual warfare. After a week or so of fervent prayer on this matter, these feelings of resentment faded. While they creep back into my mind and heart a bit now and then, I am no longer ensnared by them and know how to quickly seek the power of Jesus' name to free me from them. As soon as I evoke the name of Jesus to banish these disquieting spirits, the bloom of their darkness is nipped in the bud.

To give you the end of the story, Samuel's recovery was nothing short of miraculous. After thirty days in a coma and a constant circle of prayer, he woke up. After that, he was in the hospital for another month receiving physical, occupational, and speech therapy. It was a long road to recovery, but it was a road that so many of us feared Sam would not have a chance to walk. With injuries of Samuel's severity, according to Dr. Geoffrey Manley, a renowned neurosurgeon at UCSF, only ten percent of patients survive. And of those ten percent, only one percent can live independently.

After this injury and his recovery, Samuel went on to achieve a great deal. He graduated from USC in three years with a BS in international business degree. He obtained two MBA degrees from Tsinghua University and Jiao Tong University, both of the most elite universities in China. Now he lives independently in China and has for the past sixteen years. He is a miracle.

### The BIG Lesson: Jesus' Example of Forgiveness

Nelson Mandela said, "Resentment is like drinking poison and then hoping it will kill your enemies." One of the most important things that was revealed to me as I addressed my own resentment toward Ex was that I was living in a state of unforgiveness.

We often think of forgiveness as something that one seeks of us, or we seek from another. Remorse is felt. Amends are made; responsibility is taken. Then, forgiveness is granted. And yes, that is one kind of forgiveness. When we do wrong to someone—either intentionally or unintentionally—it is incumbent upon us to make it right, to express our remorse, and hopefully to accept their forgiveness. Sadly, not everyone who does wrong feels remorse, takes responsibility, makes amends, or asks for forgiveness. This is sometimes the hardest kind of forgiveness to grant.

With Ex, there was no remorse, no taking of responsibility, and no apology. This is true to this day, decades later. But as Nelson Mandela said, my resentment against him was not poisoning him; *it was poisoning me.*

When I read the passages that describe the crucifixion, I am reminded that as He hung dying on that cross, Jesus did so with two thieves on crosses on each side of Him. As He suffered, the full extent of a human man's physical suffering, Jesus uttered these words:

*Jesus said, "Father, forgive them for they know not what they do." Luke 23:34 (KJV)*

There, even while hanging on a cross, Jesus was not thinking about Himself, His suffering, or the wrongs that had been done to Him. (Though, of course, He'd have had every right to all of that.) Instead, He petitioned God to forgive others, even those who did not ask for forgiveness.

Jesus made the ultimate sacrifice so that all of us can be forgiven of sin. God the Father gave His Son for this purpose. And the Holy Spirit brought it to my heart how small my bitterness was in comparison to the generous forgiveness that Christ exemplified.

That morning that God spoke to me, I was freed. I was freed mentally, spiritually, and emotionally—free from the continued harm and entanglement of painful memories. I was granted not only peace from the pain of Ex's traumatic treatment of me and of my children but also a great unspeakable joy.

That morning I took my first steps on a long journey of the promise that God made to me when He spoke to me: *The best is yet to come.*

There are those who have suffered unfathomable abuses, some from those who were meant to love them the most. There are those who have endured trauma, heartbreak, betrayal, and abandonment. I am here to tell you that you do not have to be forever a captive of these memories. You may have emotional, physical, and mental scars, but your spirit can be completely freed of all harm.

To this day, I have not forgotten the abuses that Ex perpetrated on me and my children. I believe that these memories have remained intact because lessons can continue to be learned and shared—perhaps even for the purpose of writing this very book. But though I remember it all, it no longer harms me to remember. I'm no longer in the prison of unforgiveness. I am freed of the emotional bondage of the past and have completely shed that pain.

Not only was I finally freed of living in this unforgiveness, but God also prompted me to pray for Ex.

*You have heard that it was said, "Love your neighbor and hate your enemy". But I tell you, love your enemies and pray for those who persecute you. Matthew 5:43-44 (NIV)*

Now, through God's grace, I have moved on, and I can hold Ex up to God in prayer, praying that he would draw nigh to God. I could have compassion for whatever injuries or pain Ex had in his life that caused him to be as he was, and I can pray for his healing as well.

This freedom came utterly from God. Jesus won this victory on my behalf, and I thank God for freeing me from emotional and mental anguish.

The good news is that He makes this freedom available to all who come to Him and ask. If you have been wronged, abused, abandoned, or betrayed, God offers you relief from the lingering traumatic effects of these things. By forgiving (not forgetting) those who harm us, we make way for peace in our own hearts, and freedom from the anguish is available through God's immutable grace.

God gave this to me. He wants to give it to you.

**But how do we forgive the unforgivable?**

When we look to the example of Jesus forgiving not only the thieves crucified beside him but also those whose actions brought Him to His own cross, we must certainly be humbled. To forgive torturers *while* being tortured is truly a capability that few mortals can imagine, much less enact. The unconditional nature of Christ's forgiveness is there to inspire us.

But it's challenging for many to imagine forgiving those who have done great harm to us or to those we love, particularly those who have caused trauma, injury, or even death. Those who have been victims of abuse or trauma may bear scars, suffer lasting psychological injuries from their trauma, or be haunted by memories that rob them of peace.

Are those who perpetrate these kinds of harm on others worthy of forgiveness? It can be hard for many of us to imagine. And can we forgive one who has done such harm but is not available to us either because they are unwilling to communicate with us or have died?

The questions above miss the point of the kind of forgiveness we're talking about here. Remember, forgiveness serves the one who forgives, freeing him or her from the destructive spirits of resentment, bitterness, and rage. And forgiveness can be granted whether or not it is sought and whether or not we have contact with the one who did harm.

I did not talk to Ex about my resentment. He did not ask for forgiveness. During our marriage, my children and I were victims of his abuse. But in holding onto my resentment, I was remaining in "victimhood," stuck with reliving every abuse, every slight, every humiliation. The point of forgiving him was not to change his actions, his words, or even to influence him to make amends to me, or to our children. The point of forgiveness was to follow the example that Jesus gave and to be freed of the bonds that held me in victimhood. Forgiveness doesn't mean forgetting; it means being free from continued harm from events of the past.

In a November 17, 2017, Adult Health article put out by the Mayo Clinic, they look at forgiveness as a matter of health (http://www.mayoclinic.org/healthy-lifestyle-adult-health/in-depth/forgiveness/art-20047692). Here, the article lists just a few of the health benefits to the one who forgives:

*"Letting go of grudges and bitterness can make way for improved health and peace of mind. Forgiveness can lead to:*

- *Healthier relationships*

- *Improved mental health*

- *Less anxiety, stress, and hostility*

- *Lower blood pressure*

- *Fewer symptoms of depression*

- *A stronger immune system*

- *Improved heart health*

- *Improved self-esteem*

The article states what I absolutely found to be true for me when it came to Ex. It goes on to say: "But if you don't practice forgiveness, you might be the one who pays most dearly."

Forgiveness is a decision, plain and simple. We must *decide* to forgive, even when it's hard. By forgiving others, we free ourselves. Forgiveness may just be the best exercise for your mind, body, and spirit.

It is God's will that we should always forgive. If we forgive, then scripture promises us abundance.

*If you are willing and obedient, you will eat the good things of the land. Isaiah 1:19 (NKJV)*

## God's Voice is the Best GPS

*Whether you turn to the right or to the left, your own ears will hear him. Right behind you a voice will say, "This is the way you should go, whether to the right or to the left." Isaiah 30:21 (NKJV)*

Finding our way around in the earthly world has been made easier by the invention of GPS devices on our phones and in our cars. Once our destination has been determined, the voices on our navigation devices offer a route (sometimes even several alternative routes) and turn-by-turn instructions to keep us on track. If we veer off of the recommended path or choose to disregard the guidance of our friendly director, the guide-voice lets us know. "Recalculating" is the cue that we have missed a turn or gone off on a detour. Then our friendly GPS offers a way for us to resume our journey or to find another path toward our destination.

God has some similar qualities to GPS. He does not drive the car for us. But when we ask Him for directions, He is there to offer help. When we veer, He is there to guide us back. If we get hopelessly lost, He is there to help us find a path back home. Yes, we can disregard the GPS, and we can override it. We are the free-will drivers of our cars. And though this human-made device of a GPS system can be flawed, it generally offers the best options for our paths.

Of course, God is a much better navigator than Siri. He is not surprised by road closures or detours. He knows not only what is on the road ahead of us but also what we will encounter on every road, for every destination that we will seek throughout our lives.

As for me, I've found that God's voice is an infinitely reliable GPS system for how I am to live, what daily choices I make at each turn, and how best I can arrive at a happy, healthy, abundant life and a heavenly destination.

But it is not always so easy to heed God's guidance, to subjugate our own wills, and to accept His answers to our prayers—His yes answers, His no answers, and His wait answers.

## What Does It Mean to Be Pure of Heart?

*Blessed are the pure of heart for they will see God. Matthew 5:8 (KJV)*

*Create in me a pure heart, O God, and renew a steadfast spirit within me. Psalm 51:10 (KJV)*

To be pure of heart is to be living a life that is pleasing to God, for His purpose, and not our own.

It is important when trying to hear God's voice and discerning His will that we approach our prayer with a pure heart. What does this mean? It is, quite simply, accepting that God knows what's best for us.

This means that we come to God, not with our own agenda, not with our own desires, selfish needs, and not with our own egos. When we pray for the means to glorify God, to live a life of example and inspiration, and to provide for the needs of others, our hearts are pure. When we have a pure heart, we seek communion with God to hear His voice, His plan, and His desires for our lives.

When trying to imagine the purest communication that is possible with God, we need look no further than Genesis. In the story of creation, God created Adam and Eve, who lived in pure communion with Him. They were utterly free, unashamed of their nakedness, in perfect harmony with God's will for them. Life was blissfully safe. Their needs were all abundantly cared for. They had a life without strife or hardship, sickness, pain, and disease. They lived in abundance, and they were given dominion over all that was created for them.

*So God created man in his own image, in the image of God created he him: male and female created he them. And God blessed them, and God said unto them, "Be fruitful, and multiply, and replenish the earth, and subdue it: and have dominion over the fish of the sea, and over the fowl of the air, and over every living thing that moveth upon the earth." Genesis 1:27-28 (KJV)*

What this creation story illustrates is God's generous love for His children. He literally created the world over which we, His children, are to have dominion. He provides for our every need and He desires for us to live in close communion with Him. That is how Adam and Eve lived in the world that God created for them: in pure communion with their Creator.

What changed? Quite simply, it was the choice that Adam and Eve made to go against God's will, to disregard His voice, and to eat of the "forbidden fruit" from the Tree of Knowledge of Good and Evil. In a splitsecond, they fell for the crafty and deceitful serpent. They lost their dominion and handed it over to Satan, theserpent.

*Watch and pray so that you will not fall into temptation. The spirit is willing, but the flesh is weak. Matthew 26:11 (NIV)*

This is God's life-giving instruction to us.

Despite that God had provided for their every need and want, Adam and Eve disregarded His singular command, their own desires leading them to their act of defiance of God's will. It was ego, their desire to obtain that which they did not need that made their hearts impure. This act of disobedience—this sin—was how they became separated from their pure communion with God.

So what is our lesson here? The lesson is not what many might think—about a moody God who has arbitrary rules and punishes those who disobey Him. Rather, the story in Genesis is about the abundance that He has for us and how sin separates us from the glorious lives that God has for us.

We are not God's puppets; He gave us each a free will

to make choices for ourselves. He has given us intelligence, imagination, and creativity; these are there for us to use. But when we use these for our own selfish needs, for our own glory, or solely for the purpose of obtaining rewards for ourselves, our hearts are not pure. Like that GPS I mentioned earlier, God is there to guide us, always reminding us of the path of righteousness that He wants us to walk and that, ultimately, we want to walk as well. His voice does not rely on satellite communication systems and is available to us 24/7/365.

Let me offer a real-life example of when God's guidance led me toward abundance. Don't worry. I'll also share examples of when I allowed my own desires and the influence of others to disregard God's voice. Both kinds of stories are useful as we try to understand this tender topic of discerning God's voice from our own.

**When God Guides Us, He Provides All That We Need**

Much after my first marriage ended and I became financially successful, I decided to serve God by contributing to my community and to those in need. I served on the board of Children's Hospital in San Francisco (which later became CPMC). My own son had so benefited from medical care following an accident that I felt God's guidance to serve other children. And God guided me also to serve on the board of Alumnae Resources, an organization that then helped women, particularly empty nesters, to prepare for interviews, to find jobs, and return to the job market. He guided me also to serve on the board of San Francisco's Grace Cathedral and Episcopal Diocese of Northern California, an organization that is renowned for its services for disadvantaged people, and to fund the building of Shekinah Hall and seeded the Channel Television station for River of Life Chinese Christian Church in Santa Clara, California.

Music is one of the most unifying and inspiring of God's creations, and it's my belief that music is the most universal of languages. I was happy to serve on the board of the San Francisco Symphony. Part of my contribution there is to promote the annual event that celebrates Chinese New Year using the universal language of music to bridge the East and the West, which I've done for more than twenty years now.

After some time, it came to pass that the San Francisco Opera Company wanted to produce "The Dream of the Red Chamber," a major classical Chinese novel adapted to an opera. Though I was not on the board of the opera, other board members kept pushing me to do some fundraising for this event because they knew that I was an advocate for wanting to see Chinese culture celebrated. While fundraising is a part of nearly every community institution, and I had done some fundraising for the symphony, the contributions I'd asked for previously were comparatively modest. But this fundraiser event for the opera event was to sell tables at the dinner for a minimum of $30,000!

I didn't want to do this, and I wrestled with the idea, my will battling against the request. Said another way, my flesh was unwilling. Part of my lack of willingness was that I didn't want to gouge people, and the cost of these tables seemed astronomical. I was successful at serving my real estate clients, helping them to make satisfying investments. And I'd been greatly rewarded for these skills. But to simply ask for money? That was another matter. My resistance was strong.

Despite my unwillingness, God spoke to me. Clearly. He said, "You can do this. You have what you need."

God's voice was so clear that despite my hesitation and my lack of confidence, I said yes. I agreed to raise money with a commitment to raise a minimum of $30,000.

As soon as I said yes to God, it was as if He downloaded all of the information that I needed. The names of possible donors came to me, along with what to say and how to proceed. You see, God is our General Partner in our every decision and plan when our hearts and motivations are pure. He is always there to help, remember: omniscient, omnipotent, and omnipresent. What earthly business partner is available 24/7? And with God as a partner, you don't even need a telephone, a Zoom link, or Skype to reach Him!

With His divine help, I did not only raise $30,000; instead, I raised an amount that greatly exceeded that and did so with more ease than I'd have imagined. Most of my friends thought it was a most worthwhile project and were very happy to be part of it. I've since found that whenever my motive is pure and I follow God's prompting, the tasks come easily because God is my partner in the process. He already laid the groundwork for me to exceed the goal.

Next, I'll tell about a time that I ignored God's voice. You can just imagine how well that went.

## BALLOON POPPER

A **Joyful 'toon** by Mike Waters

To the Jews who had believed him, Jesus said, "If you hold to my teaching, you are really my disciples. Then you will know the truth, and the truth will set you free."
— JOHN 8:31–32 NIV

**The Texas Tower—stumbled and humbled**

In 1979, after achieving some success and a positive reputation, I was representing a group of four elite and sophisticated Hong Kong investors. They all are well familiar with the risks and rewards of commercial real estate investment. One of the members of this group was the chairman of a major Hong Kong bank, so he knew real estate financing. A second was a major Hong Kong developer and shipping magnate with expertise in those areas. A third was a founder and expert in a powerful real estate conveyance law firm. The fourth was a major high-rise residential developer. It felt like we had assembled all of the real estate expertise we could possibly want. They were looking at commercial real estate and for opportunities to diversify their assets in anticipation of the handover of Hong Kong back to China from the British.

A high-rise office building in downtown Houston, Texas, came into my view, and it seemed perfect for this group of eager and learned investors. At least it *seemed* perfect—on paper.

My prestigious clients were highly enthusiastic about the deal. Their financing was in place. I had done all of the analysis and projections, thinking myself quite clever in the process, as my investors would be able to double their investment in four years. But I'll confess that though the deal looked great and came with a sizable commission, I did not have peace in my heart about the transaction. That nagging little feeling, I would later learn, was God's work. You see, if the deal had been "right" and my motivations pure, He would have granted me peace of mind in the transaction. I knew this, but I ignored that nagging feeling of doubt, tempted as I was by the possibility of such a big deal. I also allowed my most sophisticated clients' enthusiasm about the deal and my view of them as experts to override my hesitations.

You see, this is where my real estate analysis and ability to communicate data on spreadsheets (as well as my pride) entered the scene. These four highly sophisticated, seasoned real estate investment experts also brought their knowledge and experience to bear. This would be a five million dollar deal, and the clients would spend another two million renovating and then have a property that would be worth twice what they invested with great cash flow. The possibility of their success was huge. I was skilled at my job. I knew how to research properties. I understood real estate investments. It seemed like a giant coup to get this deal. But to do it, I had to override or ignore that feeling of unease, thinking that I knew better. I relied on my mind, not on God and the Holy Spirit working within me.

I made the sale.

It was very soon after that when the unprecedented Texas oil crisis hit. In one way, this is a very similar situation to the Corona Virus pandemic in 2020. It is unprecedented. And though scientists may have knowledge about such things, most of us never anticipated the pandemic growing the way it did. The same was true back then about the Houston oil crisis. Even the largest Houston commercial real estate developer, Gerald Hines, did not see it coming. He had millions of square feet of office space that laid vacant at an immense loss. Nobody saw it coming. No one on earth, that is.

With the collapse and the subsequent recession to follow, no one was renting office space in Houston. The Texas Tower office building project went into Chapter 11 and Chapter 7 to stop their losses. I humbly apologized and returned my entire commission and more, to my clients.

If I had heeded the gentle nudging of God's soft warning, I would have avoided a disaster. I did not serve God or my clients well. God wanted to protect my clients and me, but I ignored Him.

*The Lord says, "I will guide you along the best pathway for your life. I will advise you and watch over you." Psalm 32:8 (NLT)*

Though my clients did not hold me responsible for the results, I still felt horrible. It's not that in my earthly mind I should have known about the upcoming oil crisis. No, I cannot be expected to know such things. I felt badly because the reason that I had not served my clients was that I had not served God's purposes in this transaction. I had let my own intelligence and skill as well as my client's will and knowledge determine the course.

*Trust God from the bottom of your heart; don't try to figure out everything on your own. Listen for God's voice in everything you do, everywhere you go; He's the one who will keep you on track. Don't assume that you know it all. Run to God! Proverbs 3:5-7 (MSG)*

I had prayed prior to the deal but did not hear an overt answer from God but for my feelings of unease while the deal was transpiring. Had the deal been a wise one, I'd have had peace in my heart. Had I sought and welcomed God's guidance, I'd have known that. It was when the next opportunity came along that I learned the true lesson of seeking God's input.

### God, my heavenly General Partner

Let me tell you a story about God's timing.

Some years after the Texas Tower incident, I was offered an opportunity to co-invest in a property in Marysville, California. This property was most attractive for development because it has water on site. In California, to have water on-site is invaluable. I prayed about if I should participate for weeks. God was silent. I prayed again, and God remained silent.

Finally, one day, I said to God, "Heavenly Father, I am not trying to hurry you, but the general partner needs me to make a commitment as he needs to close escrow to fund the property soon."

God said, " Margaret, do you really want my answer?"

I said, "Of course, otherwise, I would not have asked you about this."

God spoke with perfect clarity. "I have not answered you because I know you would not like my answer. My answer is no."

I was upset because God did not trust me with my better judgment. (Can you imagine the audacity of this? It seems so ridiculous now.) So I replied, "I have had a very good track record in land deals," I said. (I temporarily forgot it was God's supernatural favor that had resulted in so much success; I took credit out of pride.) "Do you not trust my expertise?" I pleaded. "You should let go and let me make some decisions and not override me. Please tell me your reason for saying no to me." I was still that girl who did not want to be micromanaged about how many wontons I should eat.

God's answer was brief, and He has a sense of humor. "May I remind you of the Texas Tower transaction?" As soon as God said this to me, I knew that He knows the future and I do not.

The Texas Tower fiasco was a pain that I had not forgotten. Through that lesson, I'd learned not to rely on only earthly knowledge—mine or that of renowned experts. I certainly did not want to repeat that experience.

The next day after receiving God's emphatic "no," I told the general partner of this Marysville land transaction, "So sorry I cannot co-invest with you because my general partner in heaven said no."

He couldn't believe it, telling me that I was missing out on the best opportunity to double my money in a year. A temptation. A test. Satan often appeals to our greed and pride. But I had heard God clearly, and this time I chose to obey. I walked away from that deal.

A few years later, I bumped into one of the investors in that property on the street. She told me that she would like to accept Jesus as her Savior because it had been so clear that my God knew what He was talking about. It turned out that the army corps of engineers had declared that Marysville land in a 100-year flood plain after the close of escrow on that deal. This meant that they were not allowed to build on it—at all. The investment proved disastrous. God had saved me from losing a hefty investment.

Of course, God knows best on all matters, even financial ones. But even more important than the potential financial loss was that my seeking, hearing, and ultimately obeying God (despite my bit of pride at first) resulted in another recognizing my faith and God's influence and finding salvation as a result. It is our willingness to hear and obey God that determines the impact of our lives on others.

*"For I know the plans I have for you," says the Lord. "They are plans for good and not for disaster, to give you a future and a hope. In those days when you pray, I will listen. If you look for me wholeheartedly, you will find me." Jeremiah 29:11-12 (NLT)*

Doesn't it seem like a wise idea to have God as our general partner in all things? Wouldn't we all be best if we had a partner who wants the best for us and will always flawlessly lead us toward our best interests? Human partners may be virtuous and well-intended, and certainly, we should do our homework in our work. But I'll welcome God's perfect direction, even over the wisest human expertise every time.

While I still struggled with pride and was tempted to act independently of God, I ultimately chose to obey and was rewarded by being spared the loss in the Marysville property. I remain imperfect, but I continue to make progress.

Can we override God's "no"? Of course, and we often do. Remember that free will we were given? When I've ignored God's guidance, going instead for what my earthly intelligence or my stubborn will led me to believe was the best, I'm inevitably proven wrong. God simply does not make mistakes. Thinking we know better usually springs from our own pride rather than from a place of wisdom.

There are times when God's answer to our prayers is not yes, or no, but wait. In addition to His infinite wisdom about what is right or wrong for us, God also knows *when* things are right for us. As humans, we are built for immediate gratification. We want what we want when we want it. But God sees past, present, and future. His vision is infinite. He has exquisite timing and understanding that perhaps what we seek from Him is fine, but that the timing is better if we wait.

It's during the "wait" times that it's easy to lose faith. Ironically, it is in precisely these times that our faith is given the opportunity to grow. By waiting, trusting in God, and witnessing the perfect timing of His divine will, our trust in Him grows as the wisdom of His answers is revealed.

**God is the best matchmaker**

While the examples I've offered above are about financial and career matters, we must not forget that God is available and desires to provide guidance on our most personal and intimate matters as well. Listening to God's voice brings abundant rewards of every kind.

Understandably, after the end of my first marriage, I was focused on providing for my children and creating security for them and for myself. As mentioned in Part 1, God's guidance led me to real estate as my way of achieving this, and God is a man of His word! Through His guidance, I was able to achieve a level of success that I could not have imagined, much larger than even I had originally prayed for. I worked toward keeping my heart pure, desiring to provide a great service to my clients and to be a glory to God. This not only resulted in the security I sought for my children but also created a generous life of abundance.

As I was focused on my career and the care of my growing children, I did not consider remarrying. My first marriage had been such a source of heartbreak and anguish that I was very cautious. I was focused on caring for my children and building my profession in order to do so.

God's timing is often different than our own— sometimes His timing is faster than ours. My divorce from Ex became final in June of 1978. In July, I met Ted Collins. In my business transactions, I often worked collaboratively with attorneys, one of whom was Ted. I admired Ted's intelligence, kindness, and integrity. I had just been freed of an abusive husband, so romance and marriage was the last thing on my mind. The idea of romance, much less marriage, was not even on my map. But God's GPS guidance arrived, nudging me to accept dates when this man asked.

I must admit I was very much attracted to him. As we continued to date, despite all of my earlier hesitations, I felt at peace with this good, kind, gentle, loving man. When Ted proposed, I felt peace in my soul, but my mind kept plaguing me with questions. God's voice came to me saying that Ted should be my husband. I did not believe it.

First of all, Ted is American and of English, Swedish, and German descent. My culture—and particularly the generation in which I was raised—led me only to consider Chinese suitors before. This was the expectation of my family as well. "God," I prayed. "You want me to marry this American man?" I did not believe God's answer would be yes.

But God's answer was clear.

Truly, I was in disbelief, not because of any bigotry against Ted or his culture, but because by the finite understanding in my "natural" world thinking, I had simply not imagined such a pairing. I had assumed that I should follow the cultural expectations with which I was brought up, that if I was to marry at all, I was to marry a Chinese man, to be with one whose background, traditions, and values were more obviously similar to my own. Interracial marriage was still quite a taboo at that time, even in America. So I was concerned about the impact on my children for me to be in a mixed marriage.

But you see, these were all ideas of my mind, of

my culture, of my earthly knowledge. They were not the concerns of God.

God reminded me, as I struggled with the idea of being with Ted, of the path I'd taken on my own. I'd married a "perfect choice" for my first marriage, using logic, emotions, and human culture as my guidance system. Ex had been a man of my cultural background. I had used my own discernment in choosing to marry the first time. I surely did not want to make the same mistake twice.

Given how things evolved with Ex, I could see that God's heavenly kingdom had something different for me. I surrendered to God's will. And, I had peace— the "peace that transcends understanding."

*Then you will experience God's peace, which exceeds anything we can understand. His peace will guard your hearts and minds as you live in Christ Jesus. Philippians 4:7 (NLT)*

I could not have found a more respectful, loving, understanding, thoughtful, supportive, kind, and wise partner in this life than I have found with Ted Collins. God made His vision for me to have a life of peace, happiness, love, and abundance clear.

To confirm that I was on the right path in choosing Ted, I was given the ultimate opportunity to know what kind of man Ted truly is. Following God's voice, I accepted Ted's proposal of marriage. But soon after I'd accepted Ted's proposal, my son was in the auto accident that I mentioned earlier. With him being so young—eleven years old at the time— and with the severity of his injuries, I could think of little else.

I told Ted that I could not think of marriage while my son's health was in the balance and that if Sam was to require intense, lifelong care, I would be that care and could not, in good faith, offer to be a wife.

Ted's response was simple. "I'll wait," he said. He

said this, not knowing if Sam's recovery would take weeks, years, or a lifetime. This not only impressed me but also moved me greatly and revealed the kind of man Ted is— one I could trust to honor me and to respect my duties as a mother.

All that was left to do for my son was to pray, and we did. I surrendered. As his mother, I vowed that no matter what his condition would ultimately be, I would care for my son.

Then, the miracle occurred. The boy that I'd been told would likely never wake, woke. The boy that they said might never speak or walk or care for himself, spoke, walked, and after recovery and treatment grew to care for himself.

After Sam's miraculous recovery, Ted was there, still patiently waiting for me. God had guided me to him, and Ted was to be my husband. As if I needed any more signs from God that this was the right choice, Ted shared something that was not only a confirmation that to marry was the right thing but also something that has become one of my biggest blessings. Ted said, "I had dinner with my two daughters." His face wore a kind expression. "My daughters both think that it's time that we marry."

These two bonus daughters and their families have been a source of enormous joy in my life, and that they chose me as their stepmother is among my biggest honors. They recognized that I loved their father, that I loved God, and that I would grow to love them and their children as well.

Ted and I have been married now for over thirty-nine years. Not only is my marriage with Ted free of the abuses I suffered in my first marriage, but I can honestly say that in all our years of marriage, we have never had a fight. We communicate. We value each other's input. We respect one another as individuals. We compromise. We share great joy together. I am grateful every day that God guided me to this unlikely marriage. Above all, Ted is a fantastic stepfather to my children. He is wise, patient, and loving to them.

I'm grateful to God for guiding me to welcome this man, this marriage, into my life. It is among my greatest treasures.

### What does the voice of God sound like?

When I say that God speaks to me, people may wonder what form this takes. Do I imagine God's voice? Do I dream it? Is His presence simply a feeling? Do I really "hear" Him?

I can tell you that for me, my conversations with God are as clear, and many times far clearer to me than my conversations with fellow humans. God speaks simply, directly, and without the confusion of many of our human exchanges. To access a conversation with God, I do not need to go to a special sanctuary or adopt a specific position to pray. I talk with God, and He talks with me, in a constant way. I often tell people that I like to have a chitchat with God about a topic of concern.

*My sheep listen to my voice. I know them, and they follow me. John 10:27 (NLT)*

God welcomes our questions, our troubles, and our challenges. He welcomes our doubts, always responding with clarity and reassurance in return. And yes, I hear God's voice.

But how can we discern God's voice from that of our own imaginations, of our own wills, or of our own desires? How can we tease out the true voice of God from the distractions of the world and the messages from other sources?

This is the topic we will explore in the next chapter of this story.

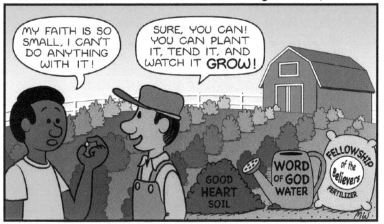

He replied, "Because you have so little faith. Truly I tell you, if you have faith as small as a mustard seed, you can say to this mountain, 'Move from here to there,' and it will move. Nothing will be impossible for you." — MATTHEW 17:20 NIV

# Chapter 5

## How to Discern Our Own Desires and the Distractions of the World in Order to Hear God's Voice

*All scripture is inspired by God and is useful to teach us what is true, and to make us realize what is wrong in our lives. It corrects us when we are wrong, and teaches us to do what is right. God uses it to prepare and equip His people to do every good work. II Timothy 3:16-17 (NLT)*

We often come to God as though we are children writing our wish list to Santa Claus, coming to him with a list of our desires, and expecting Him to simply fill up his big red sack and deliver all that we want. I've learned over time that such an approach is not seeking God's will or trying to hear His voice, but instead, it's thrusting our own agenda, our own desires onto Him, not for His glory, but for our own. But if God wants us to enjoy prosperity, joy, companionship, health, and success, is it wrong to ask for these things?

Yes, this can be confusing.

But remember, I came to God and asked Him to provide $100,000 for my children's education, and He provided me with many times that request. So do we pray to God to make us wealthy? Isn't that just praying for my desires to be fulfilled?

Let's take the issue of money to look at this lesson more closely.

When I came to God, asking for the money to care for my children and to provide for their futures, I came with a pure heart. My desire was to fulfill my duties as a mother to my children, something that surely God wants us to do and something that honors Him. I did not ask for riches for myself. I did not ask to look like a big shot or to gain the glory of others. I asked, sincerely, with the purest of intentions.

This is the posture of prayer that pleases God, and in my experience, it is the purity of intention that allows us to hear God's voice most clearly.

## God wants us to seek His will—in all things

God wants us to be good stewards of everything we are given. And it is important to remember that God is the source of every resource we have: our bodies, the air we breathe, the water we drink, the money we obtain, and even the families and friends we have. It is He who has created every opportunity, even if it is our task to work to obtain it. He has granted us dominion over all that is in the world, but we are expected to honor what we're given. This means taking care of our bodies, taking care of the beautiful planet He's created for us, to be good stewards of all of the resources He provides: our time, our talents, our energy, our friends, family, and our finances. He wants us to have power and authority over property, wealth, and health.

When God initiates something as He did when He spoke to me to go into real estate, He always follows through. What this means is that when we hear His voice and dedicate ourselves to the service that He calls us to do, He provides the resources that we need to make it happen. God blessed my choice to follow his guidance to embark on a career in real estate brokerage and investments, and the resources I needed to become successful at it came to me.

But my seeking His voice did not end when my financial worries had passed. No, I wanted to hear His voice in every endeavor, and I wanted my intentions to be pure. For example, I wanted to approach my work in real estate not with the intention of making the sales (and the commissions). Instead, I wanted to approach my profession with the motivation to serve my clients well and to therefore glorify God in the process. This meant that rather than pushing clients into purchases and sales that may not be ideal for them but from which I'd gain a sizable commission, I'd always do the research on the property that would best serve the clients and would be a wise investment for them, irrespective of the commission I would gain. Though this sometimes meant a lesser commission for me, I ultimately profited handsomely. Because I strived to always keep my clients' needs a top priority, they grew to trust me, seek me for future transactions, and refer me to others.

Rather than focus on the money that I would gain with each transaction, I instead focused on providing exceptional service to my clients, helping them find and purchase properties that served their needs and would be a great investment for them. I would practice with integrity and seek God's voice to guide me in every transaction. This is on the income side of the equation. Being a good steward is about income, but it's also about how we approach spending.

I will not say I did this perfectly. When I did not seek or heed God's guidance, the results were terrible. I learned some of my most important lessons about hearing and heeding God's voice because of the times that I disregarded His guidance. Let me share some of those with you here.

To be a good financial steward, we should obtain money ethically, invest wisely and prudently, buy thoughtfully, and above all, make our financial decisions on the basis of God's plan, not just for our own acquisition. Even when wealthy, our spending should always be within our means; this too is a part of good stewardship.

I'll share two stories here about financial decisions I faced that, despite the financial comfort of the circumstances, still required me to seek God's guidance. I can also tell you that in one, I disregarded God's voice and instead served my own lusts; in the other, I listened to God.

**The Lord and the ring**

As part of my stewardship over the wealth God has provided to me, I enjoy an abundant life. Yes. I have beautiful things, lovely clothes, and homes that are comfortable and well-appointed. I am neither proud of these things nor ashamed to tell you about them because it all belongs to God and not to me. I am merely the temporary custodian. And as much as I appreciate these things, I strive not to be attached to them as they are temporal goods, useful only when used in service to God. While it's fine to enjoy nice things, I am also careful not to buy on impulse and to seek God's guidance in every purchase. I look for bargains, good investments. I try to buy at the best possible price in order to multiply my dollars to serve God better. But though I strive to be, I am not immune to ego or desires.

Sometimes I, too, am distracted by the voices of the world or the lusts that are my own. Once, while Ted and I were traveling in Buenos Aires, we encountered a jewelry seller trading in a rare stone called Paraiba (also known as tourmaline) set into a ring. As the seller explained that this stone was so exceptionally rare that only six like it existed in the world from that particular mine in South America, I could feel myself pulled to it. It was a pricey purchase, but the idea of scoring big, acquiring such a rare stone began to creep over me. Part of me felt a hesitation, but I ignored it. I did not hear God's voice guiding me toward making this purchase. This was an impulse. I'd not thoroughly researched the seller or the stone. But the idea of such a big conquest took over me. I was prideful, and I made the purchase.

Later I would find that the stones are not nearly so rare as the seller told us. I felt like a fool. I'd been swindled. But that wasn't really the biggest problem. The much more concerning element of this transaction was that my motives had not been pure, I'd not sought God's guidance, and I'd succumbed to a temptation of the flesh for personal greed and not for God's glory.

That ring still haunts me. It's evidence of a moment that I stepped away from God's voice, when I chose not to listen to Him, and to instead make a large financial decision with my ego, and not with proper stewardship or God's glory as my consideration.

Perhaps the ring does serve a purpose anyway, as my reminder to seek and listen to God's voice and to disregard my own desires and pride when making purchases. Perhaps it is serving even more purpose because by sharing this story now, I am sharing God's lessons with others. Though I'll continue to work on hearing and heeding God's will, I'll gladly use my mistake to help others.

*And we know that God causes everything to work together for the good of those that love God and are called according to His purpose for them. Romans 8:28(NLT)*

**Saying yes to the dress**

The second story is about a beautiful dress.

As I have become more successful, I have found that this gives me more opportunities to do more for the glory of God. This means that I can raise money, support community causes, and contribute my expertise to help others. Even in these philanthropic efforts, I seek God's guidance about where I should contribute to those efforts. To whom much is given, much is expected.

It also means that I sometimes attend elegant events that require clothing that is appropriate. Remember what my mother taught me about how the "package" we present can make a difference? When it comes to such clothing, I look at this as an investment as well. I want to buy well, buy a high quality that will endure, and to buy only what I need. God isn't more glorified by a stuffed closet filled with once-worn garments.

Again, living within my means and spending in a way

that is wise, I purchase clothing that is necessary without going overboard. Once, I had a very special event upcoming that required a gown. I was looking at an Architectural Digest magazine and saw a woman in that issue wearing a gown that I found lovely and appropriate for the event I was to go to. It was also a gown that I could use for many such functions. I looked in the magazine, saw who the designer was, and contacted him to purchase the gown. This purchase felt entirely different than the Paraiba ring. This time, though the dress was pricey and beautiful, and I liked the way it looked, I was purchasing it not to simply "have" a beautiful thing, but I was motivated by how I could use this gown to do good. I felt God's presence and a sense of peacemaking this purchase.

When I wore this gown, unlike how the ring made me feel, I felt so happy. In fact, I called this gown my "happy gown." Yes, it was an expensive purchase, within my means, well researched, well made, but it was nothing like that ring because my intention was different. I was not swollen with pride, thinking that I'd won some contest. This time my motives were pure, and I felt a sense of happiness wearing it because I felt as though God was honored by my intentions and my good stewardship with the wealth He'd provided.

Each time I've made a financial investment with a pure heart, listening to God's guidance, the item has been a blessing, and I feel God's smile upon me. That is the case with my happy gown.

I have worn that gown to several functions, feeling comfortable and happy each time. But my definition of happiness in walking closely with God is different than the way that the world might define it. At one gala, as I stood in my happy dress, a style writer (such people often attend such fancy galas) approached me. "You know, Margaret," she said. "I've seen you in that dress several times now. Most gala chairs buy a new gown for each event."

Had I not known so clearly that God was smiling on this purchase, these words might have made me feel small and ashamed. But I did not. I know that this woman is guided by a different force—that fashion for fashion's sake is important to her. The world puts shiny objects of distraction in front of us all the time, whether our buying power is modest or vast. Advertisers and peers want us to buy MORE and NEW, whether or not our budgets allow it or whether we need an item or not.

As my younger self, I had to learn the idea of "enough wonton." Just because I could eat many and they were there for me, over-consuming was not healthy or wise, and God said, "That's enough, Margaret." The same is true for our financial purchases. I did not need a new dress for every event. My happy dress was already a privilege to own. It was "enough."

The true value of an item is not what it is or what it costs but what it can *do* for the purpose of glorifying God. In my beautiful happy dress, I have raised money for hospitals, celebrated the accomplishments of others, and enjoyed music that brings comfort to the soul. I have also testified about God's goodness in that dress. Whatever a style writer might have to say about it, I'll continue to enjoy my happy dress.

So, you see now that when I speak about "hearing" God's voice, I speak of His presence and His availability to us in an everyday way, on matters large and small. Learning to welcome God's voice is a lifelong practice, but one that enriches our lives beyond measure.

In Chapter 6, we'll explore more about how to invite, welcome, and embrace God's voice in our lives.

Enter his gates with thanksgiving and his courts with praise, give thanks to him and praise his name. —PSALM 100:4 NIV

# Chapter 6

## How to be in An Ever-Present, Continuous Conversation and Communion with God

*My child pay attention to what I say. Listen carefully to my words. Don't lose sight of them. Let them penetrate deep into your heart, for they bring life to those who find them, and healing to their body. Proverbs 4:20-22(NLT)*

For many people, the idea of prayer is that one should be alone, on her knees, with an open Bible before her. Certainly, this is one method of praying. Being truly alone with God, without distraction, and meditating on the Holy Word is a vital aspect of being in conversation with God. But it's not the only way to be in conversation with Him. God's voice is always available: as we walk in nature, as we do our household chores, or drive our commutes. Remember, He made Himself available to me as a young woman when I was overeating wontons. This is what is meant by God's "omnipresence." He does not go on vacation or put his phone on airplane mode. No, God is available to us always.

Many people also think of prayer as a one-way conversation where we speak to God. Charles Stanley, a minister who I admire, talks about this. In one of his sermons, Stanley said, "Communicating with the Lord involves both speaking and listening. And most of us are much, much better at talking to God than we are at listening to Him." Charles Stanley sermon, "How Can I Hear the Voice of God?" YouTube: https://youtu.be/V4ocm31RJ7g

It is perhaps helpful to think of God's voice as a radio signal that never goes off. The signal is strong. We can listen to it at any time if only we tune in. God's "broadcast" to us is always clear on His end but sometimes scrambled or blocked on our end. What scrambles or blocks God's signal to us? And more importantly, what helps that signal come through loud and clear?

Charles Stanley explains that when our spirit is grieved because we are living sinfully, that sin becomes "static" that distorts or dissipates God's voice. It is not that God turns away from us when we sin, it is that we turn away from Him, and our ability to hear and understand His words (both spoken and written) is garbled.

If it is sin that separates us from God's voice, what practices can we employ to invite and receive Him in conversation with us?

**Practices that welcome God's voice**

Learning to listen to God's voice does not come with the snap of our fingers. Rather, there are practices that help us to push away distractions, adopt a posture of prayer, worship, and humility so that we can hear and recognize God's voice. These are the simple practices I've found helpful and the scriptures that support them:

1. Have a regular quiet time.

*But Jesus often withdrew to the wilderness for prayer. Luke 5:16 (NLT)*

2. Learn to quiet our minds and emotion.

*For God is Spirit, so those who worship him must worship in spirit and in truth. John 4:24 (NLT)*

To truly hear God's voice, we must hear Him not with our minds, nor with our emotions.

God is a Spirit, and He resides right in our spirit; it is His Spirit speaking to our spirit. Receiving His voice is not just a feeling. Rather, it is a deep knowing. This comes from listening to the Holy Spirit, past our thoughts, past our emotions, past our flesh. To welcome this requires that we make ourselves available to it.

### 3. Meditate and memorize scriptures.

*Study this Book of the Instruction continually. Meditate on it day and night so you will be sure to obey everything written in it. Only then will be prosper and succeed in all you do. Joshua 1:8 (NLT)*

How do we do this? Throughout scripture, we are given not only information about how available God is to us but also how—and with great specificity—we are to seek God's voice.

*If you search for him with all your heart and soul, you will find him. Deuteronomy 4:29b (NLT)*

*Ask and it will be given to you; seek and you will find; knock and the door will be opened to you. For everyone who asks receives; the one who seeks finds; and to the one who knocks, the door will be opened. Matthew 7:7- 8(NKJV)*

Remember, God wants to be in our lives. He wants us to walk close to Him and to hear what He has for us. So, the first aspect of being in conversation with God is to seek Him with an expectant spirit.

### 4. Be humble and still.

If we approach God with the attitude that He really isn't there to listen to us or to reply, we are creating static that blocks His signal to us. Instead, we must quiet ourselves and sincerely invite God to speak to us.

*Be still in the presence of the Lord, and wait patiently for him to act. Psalm 37:7a (NLT)*

We must be humble enough to recognize that we need to hear Him, that we need His guidance, and that we cannot solve problems or discern our paths with just the use of our finite minds.

Our minds are powerful. After all, God created those too. But when we rely solely on our mental capacity to determine our actions or to gain understanding, we are using the wrong tool for the task. It is through our spirits, humble, attentive, and seeking, that we invite God into conversation with us.

They say that God is passionate that the spirit He has placed within us should be faithful to Him. And He gives grace generously. As the Scriptures say:

*God opposes the proud but gives grace to the humble. James 4:5-6 (NLT)*

### Practice makes praying perfect

Just as with many things in our lives, learning to be in conversation with God is something that we must learn and develop over our lifetimes. We can learn to tune into God's frequency to eliminate the static and to turn up the volume so that we can hear His voice to the fullest. We would not expect to sit down at a piano to play for the first time and to easily play Mozart. It requires learning simpler pieces, practicing them, and then gaining mastery over time. The same is true when it comes to prayer, both praying with understanding (in our own language) as well as praying in the spirit (praying in heavenly language). These too must be started simply, practiced, and we can gain fluency over time.

Charles Stanley, in the same sermon listed above, states that in order to hear God's voice, we must:

- Make it a priority. We must create time to seek God's guidance and approach it with a teachable, attentive spirit. We must spend time with his Holy Word (the Bible), as this is a primary way in which He speaks to us. And we must prioritize our time to make ourselves available to verbal exchange with Him as well.

- Pursue it with a deep desire. In other words, we must whole-heartedly want and welcome God into conversation.

- We must persist. Talking with God is not a one-time conversation. *There, I heard you. Got it!* No. Conversation with God is an ongoing process, and learning to truly hear Him requires some practice on our parts.

- And yes… we must pray. With a submissive heart and an expectant spirit, we must actually speak with God in both our deep and quiet moments and in the midst of our daily activities.

**But why? Why should I listen to God's voice?**

*For the foolishness of God is wiser than human wisdom, and the weakness of God is stronger than human strength. I Corinthians 1:25 (NIV)*

If we rid ourselves of the Santa Claus notion of God, that He is simply a granter of wishes, and instead embrace the presence of God as an infinitely loving father in our lives, the rewards are immeasurable. Rather than Him being a magic giver of "things" in our lives, through being in a close and intimate walk with Him, we experience His immutable, never-changing love—a love that is the same yesterday, today, and forever. We are never without His comforting presence and guidance. We do not have to be afraid. We can be freed of worry, anxiety, and illness.

*Blessed is the man who listens to me: watching daily at my gates. Waiting at the posts of my door. Proverbs 8:34 (NKJV)*

Notice that the above verse does not say that we only approach God on Sundays or in a house of worship. He is available to us every day and desires for us to welcome His voice into our lives.

God has been available to me for every decision. When I have disregarded His voice, I have experienced turmoil, unease, worry, and failure. But when I accept His guidance and obey it, I am rewarded.

It is important to note something that is obvious here—by using your intelligence, your earthly resources, and your wits, you may seem to do well in the world; plenty of people do. But God is wiser than the wisest among us, and the truest wisdom we have comes from God. While I may be able to nose out a reasonable path on my own, God always leads me to the *best* pathway. It always strikes me as curious how many people seek the services of clairvoyants and fortunetellers, astrology and other seemingly mystical practices to find out their futures. First of all, these pursuits are nonsense, conjured out of imagination and a playground for dark forces to play tricks with us. What's amazing is that the true God knows our futures, knows what pathways are best for us. We can shun all other efforts at easing our minds about our futures if only we seek God and trust Him to guide us. The Lord will always guide us and is always watching over us. God has guided me in my career, in my parenting, in marital matters, in health matters. Because God knows every upcoming turn in our paths, He is the best (and only) true guide for our futures.

God comforts us when we are in pain, leads us away from temptation, guarantees our success, and helps to keep us pure. His voice is a beacon—a guide through dark storms and a safe harbor, keeping us from disaster. God's voice offers hope in troubled times and encouragement when we feel lost. And, when we listen deeply and welcome God's voice, we can be free of the worry that robs us of peace of mind. Imagine that! A life without worry.

*So don't worry about these things, saying, "What will we eat? What will we drink? What will we wear?" These things dominate the thoughts of unbelievers, but your heavenly Father already knows your needs. Seek the Kingdom of God above all else, and live righteously, and He will give you everything you need. Matthew 6:31-33 (KJV)*

Not only does a life with God free us from the worries of everyday life, as Christians, we are also freed of worry about our eternal lives. While God, through the Holy Spirit, brings conviction to our hearts about what we may be doing wrong, God does not condemn. When we realize we've done wrong, we must certainly change our behavior. But God does not wield guilt. He does not wish for us to be confined by living in a guilt trip. His forgiveness is infinite, and Jesus died so that all of our sins could be forgiven.

*So now there is no condemnation for those who belong to Christ Jesus. Romans 8:1 (KJV)*

Worry can rob us of peace; fear is another peace burglar. Being attuned to God's voice rids us of worry and fear. I've experienced this so many times (and will share some of these in the coming pages). Freedom from fear did not start with me; it was God's promise from the very beginning of time.

*Fear not, for I am with you; be not dismayed, for I am your God. I will strengthen you. Yes, I will help you, I will uphold you with My righteous right hand. Isaiah 41:10 (NKJV)*

Today, though I enjoy financial wealth and security, I continue to seek God's input on every decision I make, financial or otherwise. I do not let my success go to my head because I know that it is only with God that this was created.

*But remember the Lord your God, for it is he who gives you the ability to produce wealth. Deuteronomy 8:18a (NIV)*

When I come to Him with a sincere desire to serve and obey, my financial choices are blessed by Him and multiplied. God created us in His image, making us higher than the angels. He wants us to have power, authority, and dominion over property, wealth, and health. By welcoming His voice, by setting aside our own pride, agenda, and ambitions, instead of seeking to glorify God with our actions, we are rewarded with His omnipresent comfort to our souls.

*This Book of the Law shall not depart from your mouth, but you shall read [and meditate on] it day and night, so that you may be careful to do [everything] in accordance with all that is written in it; for then you will make your way prosperous. Have I not commanded you? Be strong and courageous! Do not be terrified or dismayed (intimidated), for the Lord your God is with you wherever you go. Joshua 1:8-9 (AMP)*

# Part 3

## The Power of The Holy Spirit

### Introduction to Part 3

Accepting Jesus Christ into our lives is the most momentous decision we can make. In accepting Christ as our Lord and Savior, whether we understand (with our intellect) the power of that decision or not, we gain access to the limitless powers of the Holy Spirit.

Accepting Jesus gives us all a glorious and miraculous three-in-one, Trinity or Triune God: God the Father Almighty, Maker of heaven and earth and all things visible and invisible; God the son, Lord Jesus Christ, who lived as a man and understands our earthly existence in our hearts and died for our sins as our sacrificial lamb; God, the Holy Spirit, the Lord and Giver of life, who proceeds from the Father who is in our spirits becomes our constant companion and a source of the ultimate transformation and unfathomable power and dominion.

When God created human beings, they became living beings.

*Then the Lord God formed man from the dust of the ground, and breathed into his nostrils the breath of life; and the man became a living being [an individual complete in body and spirit]. Genesis: 2:7 (AMP)*

But when they disobey and turn away from Him, they are severed from an intimate communion with God. Jesus came, died, a sacrificial lamb, for us all. His death and resurrection, with our belief in Him, restores our relationship with God. The Holy Spirit becomes His holy ambassador, connecting each of us in our earthly existence to the sphere beyond the earth, the spiritual realm. This is grace through faith.

*Therefore, if anyone is in Christ, he is a new creature. Old things have passed away; behold, all things have become new. II Corinthians 5:17 (NLT)*

When we repent and accept Jesus Christ as our Savior into our lives, our sins are forgiven and delivered from God's condemnation and eternal punishment. We have joy unspeakable and are full of glory.

*Humans can reproduce only human life, but the Holy Spirit gives birth to spiritual life. So don't be surprised when I say to you must be born again. John 3:6-7 (NLT)*

*I beseech you therefore brethren, by the mercies of God, that you present your bodies a living sacrifice. Do not be conformed to this world. Be transformed by the renewing of your mind. Romans 12:1-2 (KJV)*

It has been through learning about the supernatural power of the Holy Spirit that my life has been transformed in the most unexpected and amazing ways. I've experienced what worldly sources may call "miracles." But to the Holy Spirit, these are not exceptional experiences. No, the power of the Holy Spirit is omnipresent, omniscient, and omnipotent, available to every one of God's Children in our everyday existence. Always faithful, available every second of every day, The Holy Spirit is there as a guide, as comfort, as an advocate, as a propellant that helps us to act as faithful emissaries of God by manifesting what the world sees as supernatural.

The powers of the Holy Spirit only *seem* mysterious to the seen, natural world. In truth, such supernatural experiences are utterly natural in our walk with God in the unseen spiritual world. It is through the transformative powers of the Holy Spirit that we can experience an intimate connection with God and experience Divine power during times of great challenge, as well as in all of our daily personal and professional endeavors.

## My promise

I'll share examples of the supernatural power of the Holy Spirit in my life and stories of how others have accessed this supernatural power as well. And in sharing these examples, I must also make a promise to you, dear readers: I will not exaggerate. Frankly, there is no reason to exaggerate because the experience of God through the Holy Spirit is wondrous enough without embellishment. I will share with you only the simple truths of my experience and the teachings I've discovered from trusted sources.

It is reasonable to be suspicious of those who tout supernatural powers. After all, we have seen snake-oil salesmen and charlatans fraudulently claiming the powers of healing, when in truth, they are simply fleecing followers of their money. These fraudsters use powers of psychology to prey on vulnerable people. They use actors and technological tricks to imitate the powers of the Holy Spirit, not for the glorification of God, but for their own profit.

But here is the irony: the Holy Spirit offers *legitimate* supernatural powers, and there is never a need to fake or exaggerate them. In fact, no words I can write or speak could possibly capture or describe the magnificence of true powers that the Holy Spirit offers to every one of God's children every day. But I'll try…

## In Part 3, we will explore the following:

Chapter 7: Who is the Holy Spirit, and What are the Powers That the Holy Spirit Offers Us?

Chapter 8: How do We Stay in the Constant Presence of God Through the Holy Spirit?

Chapter 9: How the Holy Spirit is Present in Our Financial

Affairs

I invite you to open your heart, open your mind, and welcome the exceptionally good news about the supernatural powers of the Holy Spirit and what this can bring to your life: strength, peace, comfort, healing, abundance, and joy.

For he will command his angels concerning you
to guard you in all your ways;                  – PSALM 91:11 NIV

# Chapter 7

## Who is The Holy Spirit, and What are the Powers That the Holy Spirit Offers Us?

While accepting Jesus into our hearts is the way by which we can enter the Kingdom of Heaven, it is through our intimate connection with the Holy Spirit that we can lead a heaven-on-earth existence, living righteously and glorifying God in our daily walk. The Holy Spirit is right there—in our spirits—to guide us to the life that God wants for us: a heaven-on-earth life of God's favor of peace, joy, abundance, health, and love. This has been His purpose since the creation. This kind of life is fully reflected in Jesus teaching us to pray of the Lord's Prayer:

*Our Father in heaven, Your kingdom come. Your will be done, on earth as it is in heaven. Matthew 6:9-10 (NKJV)*

*The Holy Spirit gives us power to do God's work But you will receive power when the Holy Spirit comes upon you. And you will be my witnesses, telling people about me everywhere—in Jerusalem, throughout Judea, in Samaria, and to the ends of the earth." Acts 1:8 (NLT)*

Here is the expression of God's love to us as He provides us with constant companionship, guidance, and yes... *supernatural* power.

In the remaining chapters, I will talk more deeply

about this supernatural power and what it means in our lives as children of God.

## Ghosts and spirits

The Holy Spirit is God. My first encounter with Him was He convicted me of sin and prompted me to accept Jesus as my Savior. He was sent by the Father to help us become true children of God and to know God as a reality in our daily lives.

Personally, He is my constant companion who talks to me, comforts me, gives assurance, guides, teaches, etc. He is my best friend.

Many times when people hear about having the Holy Spirit in one's life, they get nervous. Perhaps this even comes from the word "spirit," and that in some branches of Christian faith, the Holy Spirit is also sometimes called the "Holy Ghost," a phrase that may further the confusion because the word "ghost" tends to imply a human who has died, but still hovers around us. Images of semitransparent apparitions in gossamer Victorian clothing arise in the imagination. And when many people hear the word "supernatural," they think of séances and fortune-tellers, psychics, astrologers, fake faith healers, and rip-off artists. Naturally, this prompts suspicion.

But Holy Spirit is gentle as a dove and nothing to be feared. All four gospels testify to this event. There are a few reasons why the dove was chosen as the symbol of the Holy Spirit. This is best described by Don Steward in his book *Why is the Holy Spirit compared to a Dove.*

As we search the Scripture, we find that the dove represented a number of things to the people in the ancient world:

- **We find that the dove was a symbol of peace.** The Spirit of God brings peace and rest to the heart of those who know Jesus Christ as their Savior.

- **The Bible says that the dove was also a symbol of love.** One of the fruits of the Holy Spirit is the love He produces in the life of the believer.

- **The dove was representative of purity and perfection.** This is an apt description of the Spirit of God. He is pure and perfect in all of His ways.

- **The dove was viewed as a harmless bird.** The Holy Spirit gently works in the hearts and lives of those who have trusted Christ.

- **The dove represented humility.** This certainly fits with how the Bible describes the Holy Spirit. Indeed, He does not speak about Himself but rather speaks only of God the Son, Jesus Christ.

- **Scripture says the dove also understands when the seasons change**. The Holy Spirit, as God, understands all things. Nothing escapes His knowledge.

- **The dove is a clean bird that can be used for sacrifice.** In the same manner, the Holy Spirit has no faults or blemishes whatsoever. As God, the Holy Spirit is perfect in character.

As you can see, for many reasons, the dove is not only an appropriate symbol for the Holy Spirit but a vivid and deeply meaningful, and multi-faceted one.

In my own experience and encounters with the Holy Spirit, the dove imagery is apt because He is very sensitive. He has feelings just like you and I have feelings. When I disobey the prompting of the Holy Spirit, at first, I have sensed He is grieved. If I continue to ignore Him, He withdraws His presence from me. When this happens, I know I have offended God. When I've spoken negatively or gossiped about a friend, the Holy Spirit will prompt me to stop. If I continue, I know I have grieved and offended Him. I will have to go before God and repent my faults to bring back His presence. It is never good to gossip about others. It is always God's will for us to pray for others. Sin separates us from God, and it is through the Holy Spirit that we can experience his disappointment in us as a prompting to sin no more.

*The Holy Spirit, in bodily form, descended on him like a dove. And a voice from heaven said, "You are my dearly loved Son, and you bring me great joy." Luke 22 (NLT)*

While the Holy Spirit is indeed a supernatural (above and beyond natural) force and a presence in the lives of believers, this force is unlike any of those carnival tricks and Hollywood-inspired images. Instead, the Holy Spirit is the manifestation of God to which 100 percent of believers have 100 percent access 100 percent of the time to consult for guidance and power on matters big and small.

The Holy Spirit is a source not of fear and eeriness but of comfort, strength, clarity, and power.

*God knocking on my door—Holy Spirit works on convicting of my sin Look! I (God) stand at the (our heart's) door and knock. If you hear my voice and open the door, I will come in, and we will share a meal together as friends. Revelations 3:20 (NLT)*

When I was a child, I had never heard of the Gospel or of Jesus Christ. My family was culturally Chinese, and while my family was made up of good people who acted in integrity, and love of family, the life we led in Hong Kong was a secular life. When I was thirteen years old, a neighbor invited me to attend an evangelical service with her. The minister talked of Jesus and quoted the following scripture:

*All have sinned and come short of the glory of God. Romans 3:23 (KJV)*

Sitting there, even at my young age, I felt the conviction that came with those words. I knew that even though I was a "good girl" in the eyes of my secular parents—well behaved, obedient, always trying to please—that I nonetheless sinned, and what's worse, my sins offended God.

The idea of offending God sat heavy on my heart. I knew that I would not want to offend my earthly parents; to offend my Heavenly Father felt intolerable.

Then the minister offered a solution to the conviction that I felt in my heart by offering what was new to me then, but what is one of the most widely quoted verses from the Bible, and one that I would grow to treasure:

*For God so loved the world that He gave His only begotten son that whosoever believes in Him should not parish, but have everlasting life. John 3:16 (NKJV)*

As the minister preached and shared Bible passages, I felt a big stirring in my heart. It was God knocking on my heart's hello door. We were asked to close our eyes, bow our heads, and raise our hands if we were willing to accept Jesus as our Savior. Right away, I felt the presence of God. I didn't then know about the Holy Spirit, but I now know that this was the work of the Holy Spirit, activating me. When the minister made an altar call, I was compelled by a force (then I did not know it was the Holy Spirit) to go forward and right there I accepted Jesus as my Savior. Something came alive in me. Suddenly I sensed this unspeakable joy in me. Today I realize it is the joy of the Holy Spirit that came into my spirit. We are made as vessels to contain God. In that split second when I opened my heart and confessed with my mouth, God's spirit came in and mingled with my human spirit. I did not yet know of the power that this presence made available to me.

*If you openly declare that Jesus is Lord and believe in your heart that God raised Him from the dead, then you will be saved. For it is by believing in your heart that you are made right with God, and it is by openly declaring your faith that you are saved. Romans 10:9-10 (NLT)*

This is what many call being "born again," and that's exactly what the experience was for me; the sensations are still vivid and sharp these many decades later. I felt newly alive and this feeling has endured throughout my long life. I instantly felt the presence of God. It is all because the Holy Spirit came into my spirit. To accept Jesus as my Savior was the best decision that I ever made. It is a decision all human should make because by this simple step of faith I was made right with God. I can access the unseen spiritual world, the Heavenly Kingdom. It is easier said than done as it took me a long time to shed my old self through the transformation of my mind. Yes, I was reborn in the spirit; this spiritual baby took a long time to grow up to maturity. And I'm growing still.

**SOME ASSEMBLY REQUIRED** A **Joyful 'toon** by Mike Waters

Trust in the LORD with all your heart and lean not on your own understanding; in all your ways acknowledge him, and he will make your paths straight. — PROVERBS 3:5-6 NIV

## Faith overrules intellect and eliminates struggle

God is a Spirit. You cannot find God in your mind. But truly, it's so easy to find Him; He's not hiding from us. Just open our heart's door to God's knocking. He will come in. Holy spirit worked on my family, my father, and friends.

From the time of my acceptance of Jesus, I abandoned the Chinese traditions of bowing to ancestors and burning money to offer to them in their afterlife. I could see that these and so many rituals born of superstition were cultural traditions, but that they did not honor God.

Naturally, once I'd found God and welcomed Him into my life, I wanted my loved ones to join with me in the beautiful life I'd discovered. I shared the Good News with my loved ones. After some time, my mother and brother accepted Jesus as well. This gave me great joy and continues to bring me joy today.

My father, though, saw religious people as weak. He was a man of integrity. He worked hard to provide well for his family and gave generously to his alma mater, Tsinghua University, and to charities. He was a successful man and highly regarded by his friends and business associates. He was an intellectual whose logic was inadequate against the spiritual realm, so he simply ignored the message of Jesus. "Mei Mei," he once said to me, using his nickname for me," I will get into heaven on your coattails." He seemed to think that he could ride along on the faith of his daughter to enter the kingdom of Heaven.

Some years later, my father was ill, dying of prostate cancer. Of course, I was saddened by his condition and did not want to lose him, but I was more worried about his eternal life. "Papa," I explained. "You cannot ride into heaven on my coattails. The kingdom of heaven has its protocols and requirements to enter. You came to the United States with a passport and a visa of your own, not on the papers of another. You must have spiritual papers—a passport and visa of your own."

Then my father voiced his new concern as he lay ill. "I don't believe that any last-minute acceptance will work. It is too late for me." My father did not understand that we are justified by faith alone, not by self-efforts, or accomplishments. He made this salvation much more complicated than it is.

*For by grace you have been saved through faith, and not of yourselves; it is the gift of God. Ephesians 2:8 (NLT)*

*Jesus said, "I tell you the truth, those who listen to my message and believe in God who sent me have eternal life. They will never be condemned for their sins, but they have already passed from death into life." John 5:24 (NLT)*

I continued to pray that my father would find his way to God, that he would get past his own intellect, tradition, and heritage. I thank God that He answered my petition.

Six months before he passed away, my father accepted Jesus and was baptized. This gives me great comfort, and I know in my heart that God's clock never stops for us. He is always ready to accept us as His beloved children, no matter our age.

My father passed away at 5:00 a.m., May 15, 1995. He was surrounded by all of his loved ones, including me. As we knew my father's passing was coming, I was prepared, though sad, of course. We sent over to the funeral home Papa's favorite pinstriped suit in which to bury him.

At 2:00 p.m. on the day that my father passed away, my husband and I were resting after such a challenging day. I was wide awake, though, relaxing when a vision came to me. It was my father calling me. "Mei Mei," he said. "I am doing okay, and I'm on the way." The vision was very clear and powerful but very short, merely a split second. My father's voice was clear. And I could see that my father had already shed his favorite pinstripe suit and was wearing white robes. He was standing on a cloud, unencumbered by his earthly woes.

My parting words to my father had been that I wanted him to find his way to heaven so that our family could be reunited there one day, in eternity. Given his doubts about his last-minute conversion and how conscientious my father was, it is my impression that God gave me this vision of him to reassure me that he had indeed entered the Kingdom of Heaven.

What a gift I was given.

*Believe in the Lord Jesus and you will be saved along with everyone in your household. Acts 16:31 (NIV)*

This is a reassurance of God's promise that if one person in a household is saved, the entire family has access to salvation. Of course, my father had to stand on his own confession to God, but God used me as a means of encouraging him to do so. One saved person in a family has the power to call the rest of the family into salvation.

But this is not only the story of my father. I'm reminded here of a dear neighbor of ours, Sophia. One day I heard God's prompting, saying, "Margaret, go over to her. Tell her about Jesus Christ." At eighty-nine years old, Sophia accepted Jesus into her heart and was baptized with her daughter, Sabrina. Sophia lived well into her nineties in a relationship with God. No one is ever too old. It is never too late. In our earthly way of looking at things, one could easily judge these late-in-life conversions, thinking of them as too late, too last-minute. But no. Not with God.

It is God's will that we become His children. It is the work of the Holy Spirit to convict us of sin and prompt us to accept Jesus as our Savior.

**The Spirit of authority**

While the Holy Spirit brings awe-inspiring, supernatural experiences to our earthly existence, this force is nothing to be feared. Rather, the Holy Spirit is to be embraced. I think of my own relationship with the Holy Spirit as a super-charging power—not only in my relationship with

God the Father and Jesus, His Son but also as the means of exercising spiritual authority over my life and everything that surrounds me.

It is vital that we, in our walk with God, surrender to the prompting of the Holy Spirit. This means that we tune in, that we listen attentively, and that we learn to discern the voice of the Holy Spirit from that of our own minds and emotions. Remember, these are playgrounds for Satan, always determined as he is to put a wedge between God and His children. Satan can appeal to our minds, our emotions, and our will, convincing us that we know more or better than God. He takes advantage of our wrong way of thinking, working through our negative emotions of fear, anxiety, hate, resentment, jealousy, and greed so that we make decisions from a place of deprivation or panic rather than from a place of spiritual strength and confidence.

I used to be anxious and worried a lot. When I was in college, I worried about getting good grades. After I was married, I worried about taking care of my children. I worried about how to please my first husband. I was using my mind to try to figure things out, and this left me puzzled and struggling all the time. Pastor Rick Warren calls worry "negative meditation." By repeating the same worries over and over, we make them more and more real—we manifest. Prayer and meditating on God's Word are positive meditations.

It's important to know that while God wants us to be good students, parents, wives, husbands, effective workers, and be good to our neighbors, worry and negative thinking are not of God. It is evil spirits that plant the seeds of worry, stress, anxiety, and fear within us.

Yes, evil is real. Satan is real. And Satan wants to use these negative emotions of jealousy, unforgiveness, worry, fear, lust, and greed to incapacitate us. This keeps us separate from God. Negative emotions tend to lead us to more sin, which further separates us from God, His power, His love, and His ability to empower us.

Let me give you an example. I was a very shy girl and became a shy woman. My Chinese culture and the era in which I was raised both taught me that I was a second-class citizen—to be seen and not heard. So when it came to me in 1978 that I was to present a big real estate deal—over a million dollars—to a male broker of a most prestigious real estate company, I was anxious. I was intimidated and highly fearful. It was outside of the role I'd been raised to occupy; it required me to stand in authority with confidence, particularly in front of a man who was my senior. Chinese girls are often told that we should be seen and not heard, while our male siblings are encouraged to talk as much as they'd like.

But it came to me that if God did not give me fear, then why am I experiencing fear? The simple answer is this: fear comes from Satan, not from God. And in God's kingdom, there are no second-class citizens.

This brings to mind one of the most important Bible verses that I've ever known:

*"For God has not given us a spirit of fear, but of power and of love and of a sound mind. (II Timothy 1:7 NKJV)"*

What this means is that no matter the circumstances we might face, and no matter what family or cultural rules we've been given, fear has no place in any of it.

As I write this book, we are in the middle of a global coronavirus pandemic. On the west coast of America, we are in the midst of huge wildfires. And fear has swept our nation and the world. Of course, God wants us to act prudently to keep our neighbors and ourselves safe. But this does not mean to launch into a frenzy or succumb to panic. That is the fear that Satan wants us to have.

The news calls this pandemic "unprecedented." However, this pandemic, in all actuality, is not at all unprecedented. There have been plagues, diseases, and other tragic worldwide events throughout human history.

And God has always been there. Satan's tactics are to use the spirit of fear and to put us in a state of panic, hopelessness, and desperation that separates us from God. This separation leads us to sinfulness, lawlessness, and all kinds of tragic emotions that result in destructive behaviors in our culture.

Once I truly recognized that my fear was not of God, I cast it off in the name of Jesus. I presented that real estate offer with the confidence that God offered and without the fear that Satan offered. The deal was accepted.

Fourteen years later, in 1992, I grew into a deeper understanding of the spiritual warfare that we are all called upon to wage against evil. I was taught to cast out worry, anxiety, and any spirit not of God. I was taught to recognize the arrogance of jealousy. Jealousy says *I want what another has*. Humility asks: *What do I need to do to create that for myself?* Jealousy separates us from God; humility brings us closer to Him.

*"God opposes the proud but gives grace to the humble. (1 Peter 5:5b NLT)"*

### Body, Soul, Spirit

Before I share more examples of how the Holy Spirit has worked in my life in the following pages, I want to clarify one bit of vocabulary. Many people use the terms "spirit" and "soul" as synonyms, but in fact, scholarly explorations of the Bible by the likes of Andrew Wommack, Mike Connell, Charles Stanley, and others have gleaned that the two are not at all synonymous and that their Biblical meaning is quite different than the vernacular that most people use.

Each of us is made of three primary aspects: the **body**, the **soul**, and the **spirit**.

I was trying to explain the relationship of body, soul, and spirit to my grandsons, who were then ages eleven and thirteen. In a casual conversation, I found a simple metaphor that helped. I took an egg and showed it to the boys and asked, "How many parts are in this egg?" They quickly answered, three: the shell, the white, and the yolk. "Of course, I explained," I explained, "but it is only one thing—an egg. And that is like the body, the soul, and the spirit. These are all part of each of us."

To my great amazement, my grandsons got it just like that.

The **body** is the easiest to understand; it's our physical manifestation. In our body, we can understand only what we can see, taste, hear, smell, or feel. Our bodies are merely the temporary, earthly vessels that we inhabit for our time on earth.

The **soul** (which many people mistake for the spirit) is also part of our earthly manifestation: it is our personality, our emotion, our conscious mind, our subconscious mind, and our will. It is in our souls that we can find our intellect and reasoning, our beliefs, emotions, feelings, and memories. It is in our souls that we find our human will—the drive that determines our choices. In fact, this is where our "free will" is housed. Free will is a gift that God has bestowed upon us and one that allows us to have sovereignty over our own choices. God is not a puppeteer with us humans as mere marionettes that He manipulates for His own entertainment. Were it not for free will—our souls—our humanness would not exist.

*When we align our will with God and enlist the unfathomable power of the Holy Spirit, that's when we are living in the supernatural and when we truly experience miracles.*

Of course, it's in our free will where our biggest troubles arise as well. When we use our free will for purposes of greed, lust, or anything else apart from a connection with God, that's when Satan's handiwork can stick. The seeds of contention in our relationships grow roots and sprout into full forests of conflict. The seeds of worry and anxiety blossom into insomnia and can lead to alcohol or other drug abuse. The seeds of financial worry can take root and inspire us toward making poor financial choices or even lead us to partake in unethical money practices.

So you see that both body and soul are about our "earthly" selves.

## A lesson from an Arnold Palmer drink

The Holy Spirit comes and dwells in our (human) spirit. It can be tricky to envision this, so let me offer a metaphor that might help. I've always liked those beverages that they call "Arnold Palmers." They're a mix of lemonade and iced tea into one delicious drink. The separate elements of the drink are inextricable from one another. It strikes me that this is a metaphor for the mixture of the Holy Spirit with our own spirits—one infused into the other.

*"But the person who is joined to the Lord is one spirit with him. (I Corinthians 6:17 NLT)"*

Because the Holy Spirit is joined with our own, we can contact the Lord in our spirit all the time and everywhere.

Now, isn't *that* delicious?

## Jesus is the beginning of God's many gifts

The most crucial decision any of us will ever make is that of accepting Jesus Christ as our savior. This choice changes everything about our existence on earth and creates the possibility for our life after this one in heaven. At the moment of accepting Christ, we each become a new creation with all things old passed away. We become a victor, not a victim. As soon as we are born again, we have the resurrection power of the Holy Spirit that gives us a life of "overcoming" the perils that face us. When we are born again, we have the ability to instantly tap into that supernatural power (if only we use it) rather than operating as sole-practitioners using only our earthly and soul-ish self-effort to solve problems. Were it not for my acceptance of Jesus, I might have been overcome with the woes of my first marriage. I might have thought that suicide was my only escape. Instead, by accepting Jesus, I became one who could "overcome" or rise above my earthly situation and embrace the life of abundance and joy that God had for me.

*"For I know the plans I have for you," says the Lord. "They are plans for good and not for disaster, to give you a future and a hope. In those days when you pray, I will listen. If you look for me wholeheartedly, you will find me." (Jeremiah 29:11-13 NLT)*

When I was hesitant about writing this book, God continued to prompt me. One of the ways he did so was by putting before me many resources of inspiring pastors and teachers who have expressed some of what God wants me to share. Such is the case with the article, *I'm Saved! Now What?* by Gregory Brown. This author reminds us that, "Believing in Jesus Christ is just the beginning of our Christian life. So much more lies ahead." (You can find his article at Bible.org.)

Continuing, Brown neatly itemizes the steps to follow in order to deepen our relationship with God and to know how to act in our lives after accepting Christ. What comes after accepting Jesus? The author goes on to offer the steps we must take in our lives in order to grow in our faith. I'll list them here and add a bit of my own understanding to each.

To be baptized: The ritual of baptism is the outward expression of our salvation and a necessary part of our Christian walk. Whether in a river or at a baptismal font, baptism can be our way of saying to ourselves, to God, and to those who witness our baptism that we are people of faith.

To consecrate ourselves to the Lord: The simpler way to say this is that after we are saved—after we accept Jesus—the most glorious gift that God offers us is that we are to give ourselves to Him. To our human will, this may sound absurd. Give ourselves to the Lord? Why would we *give* ourselves to anyone? But you see, it's far simpler when you think of it this way: If God gave his Son to die on our behalf and offers us a beautiful life with God by our side on earth and eternal life after we leave the earth, how can we not offer Him ourselves?

Gregory Brown goes on to explain:

*Consecrating ourselves to God helps us walk in His way, grow in His life, and enjoy His salvation. It also allows*

*God to work in us.*

So this "giving" of ourselves to God, of course, honors God. But it also serves us, helping us to walk with God as a constant presence. That seems like a pretty good bargain to me!

Be Transformed: A lifelong process: Accepting God into our lives is not a one-and-done proposition. It is an ongoing process. Brown describes it beautifully.

*After believing and being baptized, we begin to undergo a lifelong process of Christ spreading from our regenerated spirit into our entire being, filling us with Himself.* The author goes on to remind us that in Ephesians 3:17, God tells us that Christ may "make his home in your hearts through faith."

Transformation is a lifelong process through which we continue to shed our sinful ways, learn to listen for and heed God's voice, and seek and welcome the gifts of the Holy Spirit (More on that to come.)

How do we continue to be transformed? This is about being connected to God through prayer; by calling upon Him rather than seeking our own solutions. We do so by reading and studying the Bible to gain clarity and understanding about God's love for us and purpose for us.

To meet with other Christians: Because we are earthbound humans with human needs, God urges us to enrich our walk with Him by being in communion with other Christians. By gathering a community for fellowship, whether that's in an existing church community or simply by surrounding ourselves with other believers, we can strengthen our faith, offer praise for the Lord together, and both get and give encouragement for our deepening faith.

You see, God provided even the resources I needed for writing this book. I only had to ask.

But God demonstrates his own love for us in this: While we were still sinners, Christ died for us. – ROMANS 5:8 NIV

**How does the Holy Spirit transform us?**

The Holy Trinity—God, the Father; Jesus, His Son; and the Holy Spirit—are one God but are simply three aspects of Him. These three aspects of God relate to us in different ways.

Before we accept Jesus as our Savior, our spirit is dormant. We are wholly full of sin. This is true even if we are a "good person," doing good things. It is important to understand that sin is not only bad behavior. That's the earthy manifestation of sin. Even if we do good things in the world, without accepting Jesus, we are living separately from God. The separation from God is, in and of itself, a sin. Living without God is living in a state of sinfulness. By accepting Jesus—being born again—Jesus's sacrificial death cleanses us and makes us holy and acceptable before God. We must be holy before God for the Holy Spirit to touch us and to serve as our companion, guide, and source of the supernatural power that God wants each of us to have.

While accepting Jesus into our hearts is the way by which we can enter the Kingdom of Heaven, it is through our intimate connection with the Holy Spirit that we can lead a heaven-on-earth existence—living righteously and glorifying God in our daily walk. The Holy Spirit is right there—in our spirits—to guide us to the life that God wants for us: a heaven-on-earth life of God's favor of peace, joy, abundance, health, and love. This has been His purpose since creation. This kind of life is fully reflected in Jesus teaching us to pray of the Lord's Prayer:

*"Our Father in heaven, hallowed be your name. Your kingdom come... Your will be done, on earth as it is in heaven. (Psalm 103:20)"*

**The Holy Spirit gives us the power to do God's work**

*But you will receive power when the Holy Spirit comes upon you. And you will be my witnesses, telling people about me everywhere—in Jerusalem, throughout Judea, in Samaria, and to the ends of the earth." Acts 1:8 (NLT)*

He is the expression of God's love to us as He provides us with constant companionship, guidance, and yes... *supernatural* power.

In the remaining chapters, I will talk more deeply about this supernatural power and what it means in our lives as children of God.

In the morning, Lord, you hear my voice; in the morning I lay my requests before you and wait expectantly. —PSALM 5:3 NIV

# Chapter 8

## How Do We Stay in the Constant Presence of God Through the Holy Spirit?

For the first few decades of my spiritual life, I was a Christian—sincere, devout, and always seeking. As faithful as I tried to be, God remained "out there" to me. Somehow, I just really did not quite register that God is a Spirit and lives in my spirit. I had not come upon the full understanding and revelation on this scripture in the Bible.

*But the person who is joined to the Lord is one spirit with him. I Corinthians 6:17 (NLT)*

I did not then know I was joined with the Lord as one spirit. I was still working on self-improvement to fit into God's image, focused on being a "good person," still using my five natural senses, including my mind, emotion, and will to operate my daily life. I had not learned to stop living by self-effort. I had not learned that I was to fully surrender my all—my will, decisions, and actions to God. Oh, with my limited understanding, I made small surrenders, cherry-picking what I would surrender to God and what I would still hold onto, thinking that my own will, my own intellect, and my own "good deeds" were enough. It was not a change of behavior that God was asking of me. What God was doing was not just a cosmetic change but also a total makeover of my human nature from the inside out.

God wants to "remake" us through His Holy Spirit. It's an easy process because the Holy Spirit is already in us. But without our surrender, we do not experience this change.

It would be later that I would come to understand that surrender is not a cherry-picking exercise. ***God wants and deserves our total surrender.*** We must recognize that even if we have behaved as "good people" doing "good things," there is nothing good in our old nature. We must surrender in total, and by doing so, we have access to ALL of the gifts of the Holy Spirit. Again… a total makeover.

Yes, our spirit is reborn again immediately because God's spirit is joined with our spirit. However, the transformation process takes a lifetime to shed the old life and to become closer to the substance and the character of God. Our former selves—whether they are shy or bold, generous or selfish—must be put to totally death to our old nature.

Jesus was manifested as a man on earth for a simple purpose—to do the will of God, not to do the will of His human self. This is the example that we've been given. Jesus' words here exemplify this:

*For I have come down from heaven to do the will of God who sent me, not to do my own will. John 38 (NLT)*

Staying in God's presence is such a vital aspect of our Christian walk that I'm devoting many pages to explore what it means, what practices help, and what the experience of such an intimate connection with God in a moment-by-moment way can mean for our lives. God is not a Sundays-and-holidays-only God. He is an ever-present life force, guide, and companion. The chapter is divided into three major sections:

**Section 1:** Deepening our Faith and Connection with God through the Holy Spirit

**Section 2:** The Importance of Living in The Word

**Section 3:** The Power of Prayer, Praise, and Gratitude

As you read through this chapter, I invite you to welcome the idea of an up-close and personal, loving God who is a companion and friend rather than a far-away and distant figure of a scolding, judging god. My intimate relationship with God has been the single most life-changing experience for me. Bringing God close has eased me of anxiety, taught me love and patience, drawn opportunity and abundance to me, and brought me joy indescribable.

Now, isn't that worth a few extra pages?

### A DIFFERENT MAP

How can a young person stay on the path of purity?
By living according to your word. —PSALM 119:9 NIV

## Section 1: Deepening our Faith and Connection with God through the Holy Spirit

Many try to understand God through their intellect, reasoning, or logic about the probability of God's existence or logical explanation of His mysteries. Intellect is *natural knowledge*—knowledge of the natural world. Knowledge, according to Rick Warren, is "information gained from education or experience." (*Unshakable*, By Rick Warren. pg 18). This is human vision, not the *supernatural knowledge* available through the Holy Spirit. God's infinite existence and divine love far surpass the capacity of human understanding. Trying to use our mere human intellect to understand God's infinite wisdom twists us into mental pretzels. Such is the way to anguish and distance from God. Rick Warren goes on to explain that wisdom, unlike knowledge, is seeing and responding from God's point of view.

Remember, intellect is part of our "soul," not part of our spirit. The intellect—and indeed the other aspects of our souls like emotions, memories, beliefs, and our human will—are useful things; we can use them to solve the mechanical and social questions that face us on earth and as tools of discernment about earthly matters. But it is in our spiritual selves, through the Holy Spirit and not our intellect, that we can come to know and understand God and discern His divine will for our lives. Most of the time, it is our thinking (mind) that talks us out of operating out of faith. Such was the case of my cessation of speaking in tongues for almost twenty years after I was gloriously activated with angelic, heavenly vision. I missed out on so many benefits of the tremendous supernatural powers of the Holy Spirit during that period of time. (Details to follow.)

In our intimate walk with God, we are invited to deepen our level of faith through constant communion with the Holy Spirit. Don't worry; we don't have to do this perfectly; God is patient with us. But it is to our benefit to deepen our faith and access God's infinite power.

Let's talk about levels of faith, and ultimately how that helps us access the power of the Holy Spirit.

## My personal journey through the levels of faith

In the four gospels, Jesus addressed three levels of faith:

- Level 1. No faith (faithless)

- Level 2. Little faith (weak faith)

- Level 3. Great faith (Faithful)

Prior to accepting Jesus, I was at no faith level. At age thirteen, I accepted Jesus into my heart and was reborn. This started me on my spiritual journey. But I'll admit now that for the first thirty years of my spiritual life, though I was a Christian, I had not yet fully embraced the power of the Holy Spirit. I was a believer and sincere in my devotion to God, but I didn't yet know how to walk in an intimate relationship with God. I didn't know how to access the power of the Holy Spirit. Most of the time, I still operated out of my natural man, the one my parents gave birth to and not the rebirth spiritual man through the birth of the Holy Spirit.

Even after many years of my faith, God was "out there" to me rather than close and ever-present. I had not learned to operate out of my reborn spiritual self. It was a slow process.

Level 1 faith is no small potatoes. It is better to have weak faith than no faith. Eternal life and forgiveness are pretty big perks if you ask me. And still, God's generosity is even bigger than that! His spirit comes to dwell within me. This is a really big deal. At the moment I accepted Christ, I experienced joy unspeakable and was full of glory. It was magnificent. The enormity of God's Spirit came to dwell in my little being. People often wonder why I have such great joy; this is why: God's Spirit is within me.

*Don't you realize that your body is the temple of the Holy Spirit, who lives in you and was given to you by God? I Corinthians 6:19a (NLT)*

Wow! I just did not get that God has given me a BIG gift, a supernatural gift—the Holy Spirit that lives in me. (And, of course, that gift is not just for me, but for all of God's children.) I did not then know how to access God through my spirit. I was getting by in life reasonably with self-effort by working hard. It was so until one day I realized that in spite of all my dedicated hard work and efforts, it was not enough to save my children and me from my toxic marriage. I had come to the end of my human efforts. Nothing was working. I hit rock bottom. I could not then save my marriage, my children, or myself—this was a big crisis in my life.

It was at this point that I was humbled. I realized then that even the best of my human efforts were inadequate to overcome and remedy this situation. I had exhausted my human efforts and discovered that I needed more. This called for a higher level of faith.

Level 2: Faith involves *humility and surrender*. It is about admitting that simply being good, "doing my best," is not true, deep faith. This level of faith is about humbly accepting that there is nothing good in us without the presence of God in our lives and that without Him, our acts are insufficient.

As is often the case, it was during a time of crisis and great desperation that I reached out for God's presence. During the process of my divorce in 1978, I was so fearful about the future of my children, so I reached out to God and sought to be in His perfect will. I felt afraid and lost in my earthly struggle for the survival of my two young children and myself, and I felt desperate. So I was prompted to surrender to God's will. I call this my "relatively bigger surrender" because I still cherry-picked what exactly I was surrendering. I stepped out in faith doing something I had no idea how to do. I obeyed His prompting by going into real estate, for example. And God rewarded my step of faith in unfathomable ways with rewards far greater than I could have generated on my own through my human efforts. God guided me to work with an investor who put in $1.2 million dollars, which blossomed into a net profit of more than $12 million in two years' time. For myself and my partners, we put down $50,000 and realized a net profit of one million dollars in only ninety days. This was above and beyond the natural and far surpassed my skills and efforts; it was the *supernatural* power and favor of God. These are but a few examples of the financial miracles that God guided me to manifest.

But of course, God is a generous God. He honored my new level of surrender with the solutions I needed to exit my marriage and gave me the ability to provide in abundance for my children. My faith was growing because I was admitting that I needed God—not just my own works and capabilities—to live a Godly life.

And still, I was cherry-picking, not fully surrendering to the supernatural powers of the Holy Spirit. I'll talk more in the coming pages about this surrender and how welcoming the gifts of the Holy Spirit changed my life. I was operating on the first level of faith: accepting Jesus into my heart and saving my soul. The second level of faith, for me specifically, was about trusting God with adequate provision for my children. During the divorce process, I moved from Level 1 faith to this deeper, Level 2 faith. But my faith was still fixated on the natural world.

In this kind of faith—Level 2 faith, which is all about surrender—God proves to be our general partner, good friend, comforter in sorrow, hope in times of hopelessness, and solution to what seems unsolvable.

Now I ask you—who doesn't need all of those wonderful gifts? And couldn't all of our lives be so much easier if we welcomed them?

When we read the stories that God provides for us in the Old Testament (and of course in the New Testament too), He gives us many examples of how faith is an act of humility and surrender. When he speaks to Noah, God asks him to build an ark because floods are coming. Noah is not asked to think about it. He is not asked to find a team of consultants to examine the ramifications, the return on investment, or the business strategy for his ark building. No, God simply asks Noah to have faith that God's word was true and that storms were coming, although the skies above him were clear and blue. He didn't ask Noah to dabble, to pick which elements of the ark he wanted to build. No, God asked for Noah's full surrender. His humility and his faith. Despite others ridiculing him, Noah built. Despite the hardship and the labor and the seemingly impossible nature of the task, Noah built.

When Moses was faced with armies from behind and the Red Sea in front of him and his people, God inspired him to claim, with great spiritual authority, the supernatural power that would allow him to part the waters and let his people go to freedom. Moses did not pick apart the illogic of such an act. He did not argue with God telling him that what he asked would defy the laws of physics. No, Moses simply commanded for the seas to part—and they did. It was Moses' faith and his humility combined that made this miracle possible.

It may seem ironic that it requires humility to welcome the supernatural powers, but when we look at it from God's perspective, there is no irony at all. When we call upon God, when we ask Him for the supernatural powers of the Holy Spirit, we are humbling ourselves, admitting that compared to God's holy work, our natural powers are inadequate. Admitting our smallness and our humbleness is part of accepting that God's powers are greater. When we also combine this humility with faith, well... all things are possible.

In his inspiring book, *How to Walk in the Supernatural Power of God*, Guillermo Maldonado provides great insight into the role of the Holy Spirit in our everyday lives. He writes:

*Jesus called the Holy Spirit the "Spirit of truth" (John 16:13). Once more, the Spirit is the only channel through which we have access to God's revealed wisdom and knowledge. The Holy Spirit makes known to men and women on earth what has been expressed by God in heaven [...] To receive revelation from God is to see as He sees, to hear as He hears, and to perceive as He perceives.*

Maldonado later speaks of moving beyond our natural realm by first exercising our faith in God to enter the spiritual realm and by receiving revealed knowledge from God through the Holy Spirit. He goes on to explain that it is by applying our faith in God on another level, activating God's supernatural power on our behalf and on behalf of others.

This second level of faith is about humility and surrender. It means that we recognize the limits of our human hard work and efforts. Simply to be a "good person" is not enough. In Level 2 faith, we trust in God on a daily basis as an active participant, partner, and source of supernatural power

Level 3: Faith takes us from the natural, earthly dimension into the spiritual realm. At this level, we are called to Spiritual Warfare. This is where we can access the miraculous and the unfathomable. Don't worry; you won't need any swords or cannons for this spiritual warfare and how to exercise spiritual authority. This is not a battle of the body. It's a battle of the supernatural (beyond natural) spiritual realm.

*For though we walk in the flesh, we do not war after the flesh: (for the weapons of our warfare are not carnal, but mighty through God to the pulling down strongholds.) II Corinthians 10:3-4 (KJV)*

*For we wrestle not against flesh and blood, but against principalities, against powers, against the rulers of the darkness of this world, against spiritual wickedness in high places. Ephesians 6:12 (KJV)*

This all sounds so complicated, but it's actually elegant in its simplicity: God's power is generous, supernatural, and available to all of us at any time in our spirit. The gifts of the Holy Spirit are always available to every believer. It is through the Holy Spirit that we move beyond the natural dimension of our earthly existence and have access to the supernatural.

Imagine, if you will, that you walk into a huge room with a giant Christmas tree. It's beautiful, and you're instantly drawn to it. Under the tree are hundreds of presents, each gift-wrapped and glittering. When you step closer, you see that every package has a tag on it, and on every tag is your name. You would be thrilled to have such abundance before you. You would not walk away. Instead, you'd want to open each gift and accept it. Such are the gifts of the Holy Spirit. They are powerful; they are available; they are personally addressed to you. All that is required is that you claim them.

The "gifts" of which I speak now are not fancy clothes, expensive watches, or the "toys" that children may crave under the holiday tree. They are the gifts of the Holy Spirit. What's also true is that many people do not believe that they need the gifts offered by God. They think that what they generate in their earthly lives is enough. They have food, homes, clothing, friends, and gadgets galore. But when we willingly claim the gifts of the Holy Spirit, we discover that these gifts are essential in a way that we could never have imagined.

To engage in spiritual warfare means that we reject sin. With that mustard-seed faith, we live in the knowledge that God heals us, and He doesn't want us to be ill or unhappy. In God's perfect plan, we all live a long life, healthy until it is our time to leave this earth and join Him in heaven. God is good, kind, and generous. He does not want to punish us with sickness and death. He does not want us in conflict with others. In fact, when we find that we are angry at people, what we are really experiencing is the presence of Satan's influence, and this is the time for spiritual warfare.

This calls to mind another of my favorite Bible passages. It is one that guides me through challenging times.

*Jesus said to the disciples, "Have faith in God. I tell you the truth, you can say to this mountain, 'May you be lifted up and thrown into the sea.' And it will happen. But you must really believe it will happen and have no doubt in your heart. I tell you, you can pray for anything, and if you believe that you've received it, it will be yours. But when you are praying, first forgive anyone you are holding a grudge against, so that your Father in heaven will forgive your sins, too." Mark 11:22-25 (KJV)*

We all want to please God. But how can we do it? The answer will surprise you. God is very easy to please.

*But without faith, it is impossible to please Him, for he who comes to God must believe that He is, and that He is a rewarder of those who diligently seek Him. Hebrews 11:6 (NLT)*

God is amazing! All He wants of us is to have faith in Him.

**God wants us to desire and receive the gifts of the Holy Spirit**

Over and over again in the New Testament, we are told to *desire* the spiritual gifts—the gifts of the Holy Spirit. We are reminded in I Corinthians 13 that "the greatest of these is love." So love should always be at the center of our search for how to live a life in Christ.

Mike Connell explains that God has given us spiritual gifts to equip us to magnify and glorify God and to edify the church individually and collectively.

In the article "10 reasons to Desire All the Spiritual Gifts," Brian DeWire (https://www.desiringgod.org/articles/10-reasons-to-desire-all-the-spiritual-gifts) itemizes the many reasons that we should desire and seek the Spiritual Gifts that God offers. He explains and cites scriptures that tell us that God wants us to seek all of the gifts of the Holy Spirit because this is a reflection of our desire for God Himself. These gifts are there to help us to "overcome the Satanic fear that dwells" in our hearts. Through these gifts, we gain discernment, knowledge, the power to testify about God's goodness, the gift of speaking in tongues, and even the power to heal.

So after many years of having Christ in my life, of living with a deep desire to serve and glorify God, I began to desire the gifts of the Holy Spirit. This has not only been a part of the deepening of my faith but, also through the Holy Spirit and His abundant gifts, I have been supercharged with the supernatural power that He offers. And remember: *I am not unique*. I am actually quite an ordinary person. I am not more special than any other child of God. These gifts and the supernatural powers that come with them are abundant, unlimited, and available to all.

*Now to each one the manifestation of the Spirit is given for the common good. I Corinthians 12:7 (NIV)*

This is the next leg on a journey of faith: accessing the gifts of the Holy Spirit in order to live in the power of the Holy Spirit. This is where miracles, small and large, become apparent. This is where the mysteries of God are demonstrated. It is in relationship with the Holy Spirit that our daily existence can be transformed. God stops being an "out there" God and instead, on a daily basis, becomes our:

- General partner in all endeavors

- Good friend and constant companion

- Comforter in sorrow

- Hope in times of hopelessness

- Solution to what seems unsolvable

- Healer and provider

*Jesus looked upon them and said to them, "With man this is impossible. But with God everything is possible." Matthew 19:26 (KJV)*

Let me offer an example of how these spiritual gifts have been manifested in my life. To do so, I want to share, with her permission, the testimony of my friend Maya. Please know that what I was able to offer to Maya had nothing to do with glory for myself. Without God and the gifts of the Holy Spirit, I have ONLY natural powers of intellect, reason, and good works. But with the Holy Spirit, I have supernatural (beyond natural) powers—available to all of us, if only we seek them. Every bit of what occurred for her was because of the Holy Spirit and the spiritual gifts working within me.

**Maya's story**

Maya is a neighbor whom I would bump into now and then. One might attribute these meetings to chance, but I know in my heart that it was the work of the Holy Spirit that caused my path to cross Maya's on a certain day. It was in November of 2013. She had just ended a relationship of thirteen years with an abusive man and had left with her young son. She was feeling helpless, fearful about her future, and worried about money and other resources. Maya described her state as feeling "helpless." She was facing foreclosure on her home, and both she and her son were suffering Post Traumatic Stress Disorder (PTSD) from the abuse they had suffered. Of course, I had personal experience with an abusive husband, and my heart ached for my neighbor.

When I encountered Maya that day, the Holy Spirit prompted me to talk to her. I saw that something was different about her; I could see her anguish. God spoke to me about Maya's needs. As we are living in the natural world, with basic biological needs, God prompted me to bring a basket of food to her home. But in the supernatural realm, the Holy Spirit prompted me to ask if I could pray for her. I obeyed and went to her home frequently to pray with and for her. I knew that they had physical needs, but that Maya and her son also had spiritual needs. I encouraged them to read the Bible, pray in understanding and in tongues, and attend Bible study and church regularly. It was my great joy to watch the love for the Lord grow stronger in this mother and son. I was also prompted by the Holy Spirit to reassure Maya and her son that things would be all right.

Jesus set the example for us; of meeting earthly needs and spiritual ones. He multiplied the fishes and loaves to offer the food of the natural world, and he offered spiritual "food" to them as well.

*Then Jesus declared, "I am the bread of life. Whoever comes to me will never go hungry. And who believes in me will never be thirsty." John 6:35 (NIV)*

This is what we are called to do for the people we encounter. Maya and her son had physical needs, which I was prompted to help them meet. They also needed spiritual "food," which the Holy Spirit offered to them through me. I was merely a humble vessel for this service. I encouraged Maya to write a list of her prayers, then to set it aside and leave it to God. This assurance did not come from my mind but from my *spirit*. I was so sure that God would bless her.

And, He did.

Today, Maya has completed a doctoral degree, has obtained a job that pays her well, and is watching her son thrive in the education she is now able to provide for him. Of course, these natural needs are vital and are evidence of God's promises kept. But in addition to these, Maya and her son have also grown in the supernatural realm, growing in their faith and developing their own walks with God.

## The good news about the gifts of the Holy Spirit

Here is the most wonderful news about the gifts of the Holy Spirit: they cannot be earned. That means that we do not even have to try to earn them. These are gifts given freely by God, bestowed upon each of us as He sees fit, and every believer is endowed with the gifts of the Holy Spirit. Whether or not we understand it or are even aware of it (awareness is an earthly sense, housed in our souls), the Holy Spirit and the gifts that He brings become part of our own spirits.

*But the manifestation of the Spirit is given to each one for the profit of all. I Corinthians 12:7 (NKJV)*

## Even better news about the gifts of the Holy Spirit

In addition to the power of the Holy Spirit in our lives to guide us through our daily, earthly existences, helping us battle against the misguided desires of our flesh, it is through the Holy Spirit that we have the weaponry we need to fight against larger, and more powerful forces as well.

Our biggest and most important battles in this life are not about our careers, our hobbies, difficulties with other people, or even the health of our bodies. Those are all matters of body and soul or what are often called battles "of the flesh." But our true enemies and the real battles we face are with *spiritual* enemies. It is by having the Holy Spirit in our lives that we battle spiritual forces and conquer the challenges of the flesh as well.

*Be strong in the Lord and in His mighty power. Put on all of God's armor so that you will be able to stand firm against the strategies of the devil. Ephesians 6:10 (NLT)*

Notice here that God does not ask us to fight a battle against Satan. Rather, He asks us to wear His armor and to stand firm. That means that we are always surrounded by God's protection in the battles of the Spirit. I don't know about you, but I feel wholly protected by God's armor. With Him, I'm able to withstand all opposition in the spiritual realm.

And it cannot be overstated here that as frightening as the idea of a battle against Satan may be, that *the battle has already been won through Jesus' death and resurrection.* This is an accomplished fact. He has ascended and no longer walks among us, but he sent the Holy Spirit down to us to continue His work.

**What are the gifts of the Holy Spirit?**

*But <u>covet earnestly</u> the best gifts: and yet show I unto you a more excellent way. I Corinthians 12:31 (KJV)*

The Bible enumerates the gifts of the Holy Spirit with great clarity. They fall into three simple categories and are:

A: To say something—"priestly flow"

1. The gift of prophecy

2. Speaking in tongues

3. Interpretation of tongues

B. To know something—revelation gifts, "prophetic flow"

4. Words of knowledge—present

5. Words of wisdom—future

6. Discerning spirits

C. To do something—"Kingly flow"

7. The gifts of faith

8. The gift of healing

9. Working of miracles

In his letters to the Romans and to the Ephesians, the apostle Paul also mentions many other: service, teaching, encouragement, leadership, mercy, and preaching.

These gifts that God so abundantly shares with us are not without purpose. These bear fruits in our lives, in fact, called the "fruits of the Holy Spirit": charity, joy, peace, patience, goodness, forbearance, gentleness, faith, modesty, self-control, and chastity. It is by partnering with God and welcoming the Holy Spirit's ever-presence that we bear these beautiful fruits. And we see that these fruits are what make our earthly lives so much easier, happier, healthier, and more full of joy!

## The Maturing of Faith

When I was thirteen years old, I accepted Jesus and was baptized with water. It was thirty-nine years later when I received the baptism of the Holy Spirit activated by John Harrison (more to come on that). The gift was there in me, dormant, but it was only at this time that I was first exposed to it. I welcomed and accepted it. This was when the supernatural power of God through the Holy Spirit became a daily reality in my life. It is simply about accessing the enormous powers and many gifts that God has to offer.

Guillermo Maldonado, in his book: *How to Walk in the Supernatural Power of God*, talks about how we must "move beyond the natural dimension." He's talking here about moving out of the human powers of intellect and will to the *supernatural* dimension of spirit. Maldonado also talks about how American culture tends to value the intellectual over the spiritual.

Americans tend to have an especially difficult struggle with the notion of spirit and supernatural aspects of God. They want to rely on reason, on works, on the "doing" of life. This constant need to jam God into a frame of human logic distances so many from God and brings so much woe in the lives of so many Americans.

## An example of the gift of healing

Illnesses, both minor and severe, are often blamed on God. This could not be farther from the truth. Illness is from the enemy, Satan, and from the bad habits and choices (drug use, poor diet, stress, worry, lack of faith, anxiety, etc.) that Satan inspires, not at all from God. As a matter of fact, it is very clear from the passages below that the atonement for our sin is also spiritual and physical healing. Jesus' death on the cross paid in full for our salvation and healing. For the first half of my spiritual journey, I only experienced the saving grace. It was only when a drunk driver struck my son that I started to inquire of God's healing will. Yes, it is His will to heal.

*But he was pierced through for our transgressions, he was crushed for our iniquities; the punishment that brought us peace was on him, and by his wounds, we were healed. Isaiah 53:5 (NIV)*

From God's point of view, based on Jesus' sacrificial death and resurrection, He suffered for our disease and sickness and carried all of our sickness and disease for us.

*He himself bore our sins in his body on the tree, so that we might die to sin and live to righteousness. By his wounds you were healed. 1 Peter 25:24 (ESV)*

Let me give you an example of the healing I experienced. Years ago, I was under a great deal of stress. I was working hard in my real estate business, doing what I could to support my children and honor God in that work. I was also managing much of my father's business because he was growing ill. My son Samuel had been in a terrible accident. My daughter's needs were demanding as well. I felt that I needed to take care of everyone: clients, my father, my children, my business. As a result of all of the stress, I developed a serious sinus infection. Well, not just one infection; it became an ongoing chronic problem.

My infection got so severe that the doctor first confined me to my home and then confined me to bed for ninety days of high doses of amoxicillin. I must say it did not help. Nothing helped. At that time, I learned of the dynamic healing minister, Kenneth E. Hagin. He had a terminal illness at age sixteen, and God had miraculously healed him. So I bought all of his books, watched all of his videos, and listened to him day and night during my illness. At this time, I knew that it was not in my body alone that I was fighting; I was in a *spiritual* battle.

I decided to go to Tulsa, Oklahoma, to attend a three-day healing conference hosted by Pastor Hagin. There, he laid hands on me and said, "Sister, I saw you and your faith. You are healed."

From that moment on, I was not only cured of that sinus infection, but I have never had another in these many decades since. I never took amoxicillin again. Pastor Hagin is not a magician or a physician. He simply called upon his gift of the Holy Spirit—the gift of healing. For my part, this was spiritual warfare, welcoming God's love and healing to replace the illness that Satan offers. It only required my own act of faith to know that God wanted me to be healed.

*Then he touched their eyes and said, "According to your faith, let it be done to you." Matthew 9:29 (KJV)*

## Moving from 50/50 faith to 100%

*"Bless the LORD, O my soul; And all that is within me, bless His holy name! Bless the LORD, O my soul, and forget not all His benefits: Who forgives all your iniquities, who heals all your diseases, who redeems your life from destruction, who crowns you with loving-kindness and tender mercies," Psalms 103:1-4 (NKJV)*

I mentioned earlier that God healed me of chronic sinusitis. But I'll confess to you that at that time, I was not yet *fully* convinced that it was God who healed me; I was still in the stage of half-belief and half-not-believe. Sometimes I believed, and sometimes I didn't. Sometimes I had a faith experience, trusting and surrendering to God and believing in His power. At others, I credited my own efforts and hard work, leaving God out of the whole equation. Then came an event that changed me from 50/50 faith to full-time faith.

Knowing how much my husband, Ted, likes to play golf, I tried to take up golf lessons. In one of my practice sessions, I swung hard and hit the ground. The golf club recoiled and immediately injured my right shoulder rotator cuff. Right away, I could not lift my arm. I couldn't do even the simplest things like shop for groceries. I could not sleep on my right side. It was very painful. For two years, I sought relief, going to a chiropractor, seeking acupuncture, and physical therapy regularly. After a while, I decided that these methods were not working. Finally, having exhausted earthly methods, I turned to God and decided to surrender to Him for healing—not 50/50, but 100%.

I was listening to Kenneth Copeland's message "Healing 101". He said to have faith in God, confess that you are healed, receive your healing, and thank God for His healing. I did just that. My right arm started pulsating. The Lord said to me, "Your right shoulder cuff is healed." Sure, enough I experienced instant relief. No more pain instantly. I was healed! Praise the Lord.

Two years later, after a strenuous ballet class session, I started to have left leg and lower back pain. The pain made every minute excruciating, distracting me to such an extent that I could not exercise my own faith to get my healing. Pain—both physical and emotional—can be like that sometimes. It can eclipse our view of what is possible through God and make us forget about the healing powers of the Holy Spirit.

My Christian sister, Chinga Pan, invited me to her home to meet Bill Norton. As soon as Bill Norton and others prayed for me, my pain was 95% gone. During the laying of hands, the Lord prompted me to open myself to receive the words of healing spoken over me, relax, let go of my fear of the excruciating pain, and look to God to receive my healing. Under this strong, corporate anointing, I was able to surrender myself and all the excruciating pain that was gripping me. As soon as I let go and let God in, the healing anointing flowed through me from the top of my head to the bottom of my feet.

I learned from this experience that pain can be blinding. It can cause us to hold on so tightly that we cannot surrender to God's merciful, healing powers—the powers that are ever-present through the Holy Spirit if only we avail ourselves of them. My leg and back pain caused me to hold on, but the corporate anointing released me from my own stronghold of the pain. Praise the Lord!

**Examples of the gift of prophecy**

Let me offer two manifestations of the gift of prophecy in my life. The first was from someone else offering a prophecy about my son living in China. In 2015, I attended a session where Peggy Cole, the prophetess, taught us how to activate the gift of prophecy. It was there that a sister, who was also in this session sitting behind me, tapped me on the shoulder. We had never met before. She did not know me, not to mention the story of my son. When I turned around, she told me that she had a message from God to me. She was moved to deliver information to me: prophesy from God. She said, "You have a son who was in a car accident and suffered a traumatic brain injury. You worry a lot. God wants you to know that He sees your love for Him, and He sees this, and that He is taking care of your son. You are not to worry."

From that moment on, I was freed of worry, knowing that God was in charge of everything related to my son and his healing. I used to worry day and night, night and day before this. This freedom was enormous and changed my life in untold ways.

This is but a tiny sample of the many workings of the Holy Spirit in my own life, to say nothing of what I've witnessed of the Holy Spirit's work in the lives of others. Many years later, I was able to operate in the gift of prophecy myself. Below, titled Timmy's Story, is the testimony offered by the parents giving birth to their son Timmy.

**Timmy's story (written by his parents)**

*On Sunday, February 1, 2015, right after service at Epic Church in San Francisco, Don and I met with a Bible study group to introduce ourselves and prepare for the weekly meetings (we had signed up several weeks prior). In the church lobby, as the group gathered, we were told that Mrs.*

*Margaret Collins would host us "upstairs," and we were led to a condo in a beautiful building downtown San Francisco. Soon we found ourselves seated around a large table, nine of us all together.*

*As we went around the table introducing ourselves and talking about why we joined the group, it became clear that Mrs. Collins was just as curious about us as we were about her. Time went by quickly, and the group dispersed, joyfully looking forward to our first official meeting the following Sunday. As the two of us were about to leave, Mrs. Collins invited us to see the view from her condo; she also showed us some of the framed pictures, telling us about her family. Then she asked us if we had any children. The answer was: "No, we don't. We just had a miscarriage a few days ago." Our answer must have been as unexpected as her question. With deep sympathy, she offered to pray for us. She even asked if she could pray for Don to be filled with the Holy Spirit. The tears were streaming down my face by now, and as she prayed over us in the Spirit, we poured out our sorrow to the Lord. Mrs. Collins looked at us and matter-of-factly told us that the Lord would give us children and grandchildren of our own. She explained that sometimes the Lord downloads information to her. I did not doubt that God could speak through her. What surprised me most was that Mrs. Collins specifically mentioned "your own." She had no idea that we had already spent several years and tens of thousands of dollars on medical procedures and that we were advised by a medical director at Stanford to consider saving up for adoption. Having children of our own seemed as impossible—then in our early forties—as Abraham and Sarah having a son in their nineties.*

*It was now past noon, and Mrs. Collins graciously invited us to lunch at a nearby restaurant. She shared with us how God had answered many of her prayers over the years, and we also shared our faith stories. With renewed faith and hope, we parted ways.*

*In March, we were in a service at another church, and the Lord spoke through a prophet that God would heal my heart, and my life will have a new start. My sister, upon hearing about it, immediately said: God will give you a baby.*

*In late July, we got some promising news from the Stanford clinic—the lab results were looking great! By late November, the clinic confirmed that we were expecting! The next February, a year after meeting Mrs. Collins, we were ready to share the good news with family and friends. Everyone was thankful to God for His great gift.*

*On July 23, 2016, we were blessed with a healthy and lively baby boy! Today Timmy is an ordinary preschooler with an extraordinary story. He knows that God created him in answer to many prayers. Don and I now fully understand how God's word can become flesh: what was only a word on February 1, 2015, is now a little boy, full of life and curiosity.*

*He gives the childless woman a family, making her a happy mother. Praise the Lord! Psalm 113:9 (NLT)*

**Don't sweat the small stuff**

The examples I've offered so far to show the power of the Holy Spirit are what one might call of the "large" variety: healing of a debilitating chronic infection, healing of my son's illness, seeing others accepting Jesus into their hearts even when they've long been resistant, and a childless couple being able to conceive after God told me they would. When I say that God, through the Holy Spirit, is available to partner with you in your everyday life, I don't just mean for these large issues. He is there for us in our mundane challenges as well.

It's often small distractions that can keep us from living wholly: lost items, car trouble, or conflicts with a coworker or family member. God wants our lives to run smoothly, without such distractions, as we are more potent servants of His will without such things in our lives. And while no matter is too large for God, it is equally true that our concerns are not too small for Him either. We are precious to our Heavenly Father, so very precious that He knows and wants to be involved in every area of our lives.

*Indeed, the very hairs on your head are all numbered. Luke 12:7 (NIV)*

A Father who knows the number of hair on our heads does not want His children to struggle with the distractions of life. I'll offer what may seem like a silly example. After wearing it, I was recently unable to find a special necklace. I practically turned my house upside down, looking for it. Because I'm human and flawed, I allowed the distraction of the necklace to occupy my mind. I was sure it was in my San Francisco home. Even after I'd looked everywhere, I found myself continuing to reexamine the places I'd already looked. Thoughts of it occupied my mind, keeping me from focusing on other, more important matters.

Finally, I got quiet, and I heard God's voice. "The necklace is in the Sonoma house, Margaret." I had been so very sure that the necklace was in San Francisco. My mind was so locked into that thought. But sure enough, when I went to the other home, the necklace was exactly where God told me it would be.

A necklace is an unimportant thing. This example is not about a treasure hunt. I share it to show you that God is omnipresent, made available to us in every moment of our lives through the presence of the Holy Spirit. Whether it's a lost necklace, the nightmare of a child who is gravely ill with a traumatic brain injury, or a financial matter, God is available. *God is available to us 24/7/365. He and the Holy Spirit never take a day or even a moment off.*

**Staying in the constant presence of God**

In today's modern world, we can scarcely go anywhere without seeing someone either speaking on their phones or staring at them. At bus stops, at dinner tables, even sometimes at the movies! Humans can feel so alone and isolated, and I wonder if the modern obsession with social media is simply a symptom of our spiritual isolation. As humans, we can feel vulnerable and so alone. With the absence of God in our lives, this loneliness is not just human angst; it is a deep void.

We are created to live in an intimate relationship and communication with God through our spirits. The void created by the absence of God cannot be filled with money, prestige, status, entertainment, or material belongings, and certainly not with Facebook posts and Twitter feeds. Some go out searching to fill their void by drinking, carousing, spending, and being promiscuous. And for a moment, the distraction of these things may feel like they fill this void. But as soon as the noise dies down, the void reappears. This void is a lack of the deepest spiritual longing for God. We are created by God to live in an intimate relationship with our creator, and without this intimacy, we will inevitably have a deep sense of emptiness. *Nothing fills that void but God's presence.*

With God, through the Holy Spirit, I always have someone with me. I am never alone, never lonely. While I may enjoy the company of fellow humans—after all, we are earthly beings—my deepest need for companionship is not an earthly need. It is the presence of and the constant companionship of the Holy Spirit that satisfies my deepest needs. With the presence of the Holy Spirit, I have a ready-made best friend, confidante, companion, champion, comforter, and guide.

In matters large and small, in times of celebration and times of sorrow, when we feel close to God, and when we feel far from Him—remember, "feelings" are part of our souls, not our spirits—the Holy Spirit is right there. More reliable than our iPhones, the Holy Spirit does not require a charging cord, electricity, or a functioning Internet for us to have access. We don't need to upgrade our wireless plans or buy an app to beckon the Holy Spirit. He is always in us—no device required.

To live in God's presence is not a weekly effort to take place on Sunday mornings alone. It is not even just a daily practice of prayers in the morning and at bedtime. The most beautiful, bountiful, and glorious lives are available to us all by being in the constant presence of God.

Prayer and meditating on the Bible first thing in the morning is the way to set ourselves right, to arm ourselves for the spiritual warfare that we will face every day.

## Section 2: The importance of being in The Word

Here's a simple but important truth: *If we do not think as God thinks, we will not be able to do what God wants us to do.*

So that begs the question: How can we, mere humans, think like God? As always, the Bible provides the answers to this question, and indeed, the Bible itself is the answer to this question.

*All scripture is inspired by God and is useful to teach us what is <u>true</u> and to make us realize what is wrong in our lives. It corrects us when we are wrong and teaches us when we are right. II Timothy 3:17 (NLT)*

## The power of words and The Word

I've often referred in this book to the creation story in Genesis because it is so rich with lessons for us, even in modern-day life. This is also a demonstration of how important it is to not only read the Bible but also study it. Each passage has many layers of information, inspiration, and layers of communication from God to us, His children. When I read Genesis early in my Christian walk, I learned one lesson from it. As I've grown and sought the teachings of those deeply knowledgeable of the Bible, I've studied some of the same passages, only to discover deeper truths that fortify my Christian walk and offer me direction, comfort, and understanding of God.

We learned from Genesis chapter 3 that sin entered the world through the first humans. Though created in the perfect image of God, flawless, shameless, and sinless, sin entered. How did it enter? It entered through Satan's temptation casting doubt on God's words in the *human* mind.

Adam and Eve messed up. They forgot what God told them, which was God's spoken word, the specific instructions He gave to them. When tempted to do something other than what He'd said, they did not double-check with God and did not memorize exactly what God had said to them. Satan, through a serpent, took advantage of their ill-preparedness and cast doubt in their minds by asking Eve, "Has God indeed said…?" And rather than rely on what her Creator had told her or even seek God (who was readily available to her) to double-check His instructions, Eve instead started to reason with Satan. Adam was complacent as well. He should have checked with God before he let Eve talk him into eating the forbidden fruit.

Why is this Bible story important? The same principle applies in our walk with God today. To walk in God's perfect will, we must remember *accurately* what God has said. We must know His words and have them committed to memory, readily available in our hearts so that when we are confused, or lost, or tempted, we have the words at the ready. This is hard because we are forgetful, and we are easily distracted. That is why David said in his psalm to the Lord:

*How can a young person stay pure? By obeying your word. I have tried hard to find you—don't let me wander from your commands. I have hidden your word in my heart, that I might not sin against you. Psalms 119:9-11 (NLT)*

It is of vital importance that we "hide God's words in our hearts and minds"—in other words, commit them to memory. Adam and Eve sinned because they did not do this. When temptation came to them, they were easily manipulated. It is important that we read, study, and commit to memory God's words so that not only we may not sin against Him, but also we will live a life that is pleasing to Him. Obedience to God ALWAYS brings God's blessings.

## Renewing our minds

*Don't copy the behavior and customs of this world, but let God transform you into a new person by changing the way you think. Then you will learn to know God's will for you, which is good and pleasing and perfect. Romans 12:2 (NLT)*

My mind, my thinking, and even how I once looked at the world have been formed and trained through centuries of Chinese tradition, philosophy, culture, and heritage training. This cultural thinking is quite different from God's thinking. For me, it once meant that my mind was quite muddled up, confused, cluttered with worldly philosophies, values, and even superstitions. Whoever you are, whatever your culture, upbringing, and influences, your mind too is "of this world." In order for us to "think like God thinks," we need to *renew* our minds.

How do we do this? By returning to God throughBible study, reading, meditating, prayer in understanding (in our own language), and prayer through speaking in tongues (in angelic language). I'll cover more on this shortly.

Bible study and prayer are not homework to be dreaded; they are opportunities to commune with God, renew our spirits, and gain an understanding of how to live a life that is rich and joyful while also being pleasing to God. Like a good exercise program for the body, creating a daily practice of reading, studying the Bible, and prayer is an exercise for our spiritual selves, making us stronger and fitter with each session. Some physical exercise can be done on our own, perhaps a walk or stretching. But sometimes we need more, a good Zumba or aerobics class, maybe even Pilates with a skilled instructor. This is the same with Bible study. We do what we can on our own, but we also attend classes, lectures, sermons, and conferences led by wise ministers and biblical scholars so that we are stretched beyond what we can do on our own.

It takes a little practice at first to build studying the

Bible as a habit, but the payoff in strength for our spiritual muscles is worth the effort it requires. I'm repeating a scripture I mentioned earlier for emphasis:

*All scripture is inspired by God and is useful to teach us what is <u>true</u> and to make us realize what is wrong in our lives. It corrects us when we are wrong and teaches us when we are right. II Timothy 3:16 (NLT)*

A vital part of being in God's presence is establishing and maintaining a deep relationship with the Bible. The Bible is not just a book to be read as one might read a novel or a textbook. The Bible is a book that is rich with God's never-ending lessons, deep spiritual messages, reassurances of faith, and instructions for living. It deserves study, memorization, and thoughtful contemplation. If you memorize verses, they are there for you in times of need, and the Holy Spirit will prompt you to recall them. Even Jesus used Bible verses to answer back against the three temptations that Satan thrust upon him after He was baptized and during His time of fasting when he was most vulnerable. In the longer passage below, I invite you to not just read but to devote your concentration to what Jesus endures and how He uses the scriptures as weaponry against his demonic foe. This is an example of spiritual warfare.

*Then Jesus was led by the Spirit into the wilderness to be tempted by the devil. After fasting forty days and forty nights, he was hungry. The tempter came to him and said, "If you are the Son of God, tell these stones to become bread." Jesus answered, "It is written: Man shall not live on bread alone, but on every word that comes from the mouth of God". Then the devil took him to the holy city and had him stand on the highest point of the temple. "If you are the Son of God," he said, "throw yourself down for it is written: 'He will command his angels concerning you and they will lift you up in their hands, so that you will not strike your foot against a stone.'" Jesus answered him, "It is also written: 'Do not put the Lord your God to the test.'" Again, the devil took him to a very high mountain*

142

*and showed him all the kingdoms of the world and their splendor. "All this I will give you," he said, "if you will bow down and worship me." Jesus said to him, "Away from me, Satan! For it is written: 'Worship the Lord your God, and serve him only.'" Then the devil left him and the angels came and attended him. Matthew 4:1-11 (NIV)*

Jesus, here *fully* human, was subject to the same temptations as we all are. While He was vulnerable, hungry, and facing what He knew would be the ordeal of His crucifixion, Satan—always the opportunistic tempter who kicks us when we are down—saw fit to attack. These are the same temptations that we all face: appeals to our greed, our pride, and offers of great, though completely false, rewards. But Jesus used the scriptures as His weaponry against temptation.

When you study the Bible, you'll soon see that while Satan is wily, He has a pattern for the way that he tempts us: He casts doubt. He plants a deception (in the case of Jesus' temptation, by misquoting scripture), and He offers a quick fix.

Satan will always try to give us the impression that God cannot be fully trusted. Having a storehouse of memorized verses helps us recognize Satan's lies. Using God's Word is the best way to avoid temptation. Establishing a pattern of not only reading the Bible but also engaging in deep and thoughtful study of it has been one of my primary practices for staying close to God and understanding how He wants me to live.

If you're fortunate enough to have a local church community that offers a scholarly exploration of the Bible, I urge you to take advantage of it. As I write this book, we are in the time of the COVID pandemic; gathering in person to study the Bible or to worship together may be unwise and unsafe. (God takes care of us, and we can be safe, but He also wants us to behave wisely.)

The good news is that modern technology (such as YouTube, Zoom, and Skype) has made it so easy that anyone with Internet access can avail themselves of deep, scholarly, and inspiring Bible study and lessons from learned ministers of God's Kingdom.

I've included a list of resources in the Appendix of this book that includes some of the ministries that I've found most helpful. What is beautiful about the modern age is that the Internet has made scholarly Bible study accessible to us all, even those of us who have limited mobility or live in remote locations. We can even meet as Bible study groups using Zoom or Skype or some other video platform. There are more ways than ever to spend time with fellow Christians studying God's Holy Word.

**But I know Bible stories, so must I *study* the Bible?**

The Bible isn't just a book of stories to be read like a book of pretty words; it is God's Holy Word and full of infinite wisdom. You can read a Bible passage or hear a biblical story at one point in your life and gain a piece of understanding, meaning, or inspiration from it. But you can read and study that same passage or listen to a wise sermon about that passage at another phase of life and glean an entirely new level of understanding, wisdom, and guidance from it.

Having a daily devotion to read and meditate upon God's Word is a crucial part of staying connected to God and learning how best to live and how best to glorify Him. Learning from those ministers of God who have studied the Bible is a way to amplify what we can learn from reading it. That's why I'm citing so many skilled ministers throughout this book.

It is also of immeasurable value to have a committed Bible study group—or even more than one—if you can. Whether you gather in person or via video chat, sharing exploration of the Word with fellow Christians can help to illuminate the meaning, and therefore increase understanding, of what you're studying. Just like when we are in school, a study group supports our learning, so too does a committed Bible study group support our understanding of biblical teaching. I participate in at least two and up to four weekly Bible fellowships. My Monday group includes about twenty-five people, and we study with the teachings of biblical experts, most recently Pastor Rick Warren's "Financial Fitness" program—a study devoted to biblical principles regarding money—which I've referenced in this book. Bible Study Fellowship (BSF) is a comprehensive global organization that offers free Bible study fellowship in countries all over the world. My Tuesday evening Bible study group focuses on their teachings. Again, these are free and available in thirty-five countries, including specific groups for women, men, and children. It was in my women's group that we've been studying Genesis, which has offered me so many insights I've shared in this book.

These, and other Bible study groups, have helped me grow more mature in my relationship with God and have helped me to testify with a more precise understanding about so many factors in everyday life.

**The deeper meaning of the Creation Story**

Almost any child who's gone to Sunday school has heard the creation story of Adam and Even in the Garden of Eden. The creation story in Genesis chapters 1 and 2 is the most vivid demonstration of God's glory, power, and generosity. By simply speaking, God created heaven and earth, and all that exists. He created abundance and created humans to enjoy it, to have dominion over it, and to rule the earth. God blessed us with beauty and abundance, offering humans a life without sickness, toil, or pain. As I've mentioned prior, God did not make a measly garden; no, He made Eden—a place bountiful and beautiful for all humans to enjoy and to have dominion over. This means that we are to use all that is created, to take care of it, and to enjoy it. They would have the triune God available to them every moment of their lives. This is evidence of how He wants to bless us.

But there is more to be learned from the story of Adam and Eve beyond what a child can understand.

As the first two chapters of Genesis are among the most beautiful and glorious stories of the Bible, Genesis,

Chapter 3 is among the Bible's most tragic and sad chapters because this is the moment when the earth became a fallen kingdom. In short, Adam and Eve blew it, and they blew it big time. While God gave them everything they could possibly ever want, He commanded only one thing of them, that they not eat the fruit of the Tree of Knowledge of Good and Evil. But Eve failed to memorize God's instructions. So when Satan tempted her with the fruit, he was able to confuse her that God had not told them that eating this fruit was against His will, that doing so would bring sorrow and death. And Adam, who could also have memorized what God had told them, did not correct Eve. Adam stood by passively, and then he took a bite of the fruit. They did not take God's command seriously.

*Heaven and Earth can pass away, but my words will never pass away. Matthew 24:35 (NIV)*

When God says something, when He gives a commandment, that's it. He is not like a parent that can be talked out of His instructions to His children. We must obey.

Genesis Chapter 3, and all the way to the book of Revelation, would not exist had it not been for Adam and Eve's disobeying God's commandments. The entirety of human suffering, illness, shame in nakedness, and death are a result of that fall. And the fall was because Adam and Eve doubted God's words and disobeyed Him. And Satan is still at work today, doing the same things, casting doubt on God's Word, playing the same tricks upon us over and over again.

But the instructions are the same: study God's Word, obey His commandments, and listen to His voice. This is how to stay close to God.

*Then the man and his wife heard the sound of the Lord as He was walking in the garden in the cool of the day, and they hid from the Lord among the trees of the garden. But the Lord called to the man, "Where are you?" He answered, "I heard you in the garden and I was afraid because I was naked; so I hid." And He said, "Who told you that you were naked? Have you eaten from the tree that I commanded you not to eat from?" Genesis 3:8-11 (NIV)*

Notice that after they sinned, Adam and Eve hid from God. Prior to their sin, they had constant access to the Heavenly Father. But after, they hid because they were suddenly ashamed of their nakedness, which had previously been no cause for shame. Then they played the "blame game," trying to attribute their sinfulness to each other and to Satan. But each of them was responsible for their own sin, and their sin separated them from God and from each other. This set up the rest of the world and all of our existence to be harder; to have disease, sickness, death, pain in childbirth, and every other kind of ill. Were it not for this "original sin," the rest of the Bible would not exist; we would simply be living in Eden.

They ate from the Tree of Knowledge of Good and Evil. They were born sinless but opted to sin, to disobey their creator. The damage inflicted by this sin cannot be overstated. The tragedy of sin for the whole history of humanity is in our everyday lives, echoing loudly and sorrowfully. Into the glorious and flawless world God had created, evil, sickness, and death entered. Pain in childbirth, the toil of the body, and struggle, all resulted because sin was welcomed into the world that God had so generously endowed to His children.

Why do I tell you this story here? The story itself tells us that sin separates us from God. The more we can shun sin, the easier it is to feel God's presence, hear His voice, and receive His blessings. This chapter—and in reality, this whole book—is all about staying in the constant presence of God and all of the blessings that this can bring us. While none of us is without sin, we can strive to be righteous; we can set our lives up to limit temptations. We can choose not to succumb to the temptations of the world and pray for God's help to do so.

I also tell the story here to illustrate that merely reading the creation story once can teach us one lesson, but studying it and learning from others who have studied it, can give us a deeper and more meaningful understanding as we grow in our walk with the Lord.

In the previous pages, I spoke of how Satan tempted Jesus—the pattern of temptation that he used and how Jesus used scripture (God's words) as his weaponry against the devil's wily ways. The serpent did exactly the same things to Eve, including the ultimate temptation that should she eat of the Tree of the Knowledge of Good and Evil that she would be "like God." Unfortunately for all of humanity, Eve, and later Adam as well, had not committed God's words to memory. (Of course, God's words were then directly spoken to Adam and Eve, not yet written as scripture.) Nor did they go back to ask God what He'd meant by His commandment that they not eat of this one tree though God had made Himself completely available to their calls. So, they, without the armament of God's words, fell prey to Satan's influence.

Let me remind you of an example of my own failure to avoid temptation as well as my failure to seek God's guidance. I've mentioned in earlier chapters about that terrible deal I made for the Texas Towers. I didn't just impulsively encourage my clients to invest in that property; instead, I did a huge amount of research. I had four elite clients, highly knowledgeable about such real estate investments. I had spreadsheets and documents all that said that this would be a highly lucrative deal, more than I could ever hope for. I overrode my inner voice, the voice of the Holy Spirit that would not give me peace about the deal. I relied upon my own skills, the knowledge of earthly experts, and indeed, my pride and vanity came into play; I wanted to impress my VIP clients. The appeal of a big win was my carrot of temptation.

As always, when we disregard God's promptings, we are setting ourselves up for disaster.

148

### God's Word is my melatonin and Ambien

My friends are always amazed that I go to bed early and sleep at least eight hours a night. But this was not always the case for me. I am happy to share with you my secret to a good night's sleep.

For years, especially when I was very stressed or overworked, I had trouble going to sleep or staying asleep. It was hard to calm myself, to get still, quiet, and peaceful enough to fall into slumber. But sleep is so essential to my functioning that I would take melatonin or Ambien to help me. Ever since I started the habit of listening to audio Bible or Christian audiobooks before going to bed, I no longer have difficulty in falling asleep. It is not that hearing and reading the Bible and other Christian books is boring, not at all. It's that there is always peace and comfort to be found in God's Word. When I listen to them at bedtime, not only do I fall asleep easily, if I do wake up at night, I can just turn on the audio again and will have no trouble falling back to sleep.

God's words bring comfort, hope, and ease even my most troubling stresses. Now, doesn't this sound like a better option than sleeping pills? I'd vote a great big yes on that. And of course, God's Word also offers comfort from our daytime worries as well.

## Section 3: The Power of Prayer, Praise, and Gratitude

We may have many images of prayer: a child kneeling at bedside, hands folded with eyes closed, a believer in a pew before an altar with head bowed; a soldier in a foxhole begging God for protection. Yes, these can be examples of deep and meaningful prayer. Yet, these images are only part of the picture. In the previous pages, you've read about being in God's presence in your daily walk. When God becomes your intimate companion, you will not ignore Him as you go through your day; instead, you can be in constant conversation with Him. When you've welcomed God and learn to recognize His voice, God is not like an occasional visitor in your home—He is the closest and most intimate kind of roommate you can imagine. He is ever-present, always available, and always pleased to hear from you.

### The power of morning prayers

In lots of movies, we see the image of people kneeling at their bedside just before they go to sleep. And, of course, any time we pray is good. While it's always good to give thanks and talk to God any time, I find that if I wait until the end of the day that perhaps by then, my day has already unfolded and been off-track. I find that when I pray first thing in the morning, I align myself with God and His purpose for me. I ask, "God, what do you want me to do?" I thank Him for my good health, for the beautiful day. I surrender the day to God. "You are the Creator, and I'm the creature; what can I do today to make an impact for your Kingdom? How do I advance your Kingdom?"

To get myself into a posture of worship, I'll often begin with singing or listening to worship songs, some of which I've mentioned earlier. Music is such a universal language, and worship music can help us ascend from our circumstances into communion with our Heavenly Father.

Sometimes during this morning prayer, when I'm listening well, God gives me very specific "marching orders" for the day. He tells me what calls to make, what tasks to do.

He often puts the thoughts of people into my mind whom I'd never have thought to call on my own. I've learned to heed these promptings, as God knows who needs to hear from me, who might need help or understanding, or care. God gives me a little nudge to check in on them, and invariably I find that though these people did not expect my calls, they are blessed by them. This is God's work, not my own.

In these morning prayers, God also often directs my attention to specific readings, sermons, or scriptures He wants me to observe. Hear me carefully here; God speaks very specifically when he does this. One morning, the Lord spoke directly, telling me to read from *Authority from God: How and Why you Can Kick the Devil Out of Your life*, by Randy Clark. Even more specifically than that, He prompted me to read chapters 10, 11, and 12. While I did not yet understand why I was being led to these chapters, God knew (and I would come to understand later) that I needed to have a deeper understanding of the word "dominion" to more thoroughly comprehend how we can claim authority and power in preparation for my Tuesday women BSF Bible study where understanding this brought great comfort to our members who were struggling.

Let me offer another example. Remember the story I shared earlier about God prompting me to raise money for the symphony for the production of the Chinese opera production of "Dream of the Red Chamber?" I was on the board of the symphony, not the opera. And I felt an allegiance there, so I was unsure why I was being asked to raise money for a completely different organization. While I certainly wanted the event to happen and to celebrate Chinese culture, I didn't want to do the fundraising, not because I was being lazy, but because it was asking for large donations, which I feared would look like gouging my friends. And I really had no idea which people to ask or how to do it. But when God prompted me, I surrendered. As soon as I submitted and told God I would obey His directions, it was as if God "downloaded" all of the names of people I was to call. He asked me to do something, I obeyed, and He gave me the means to do what He'd asked. God made me successful in raising more money than I could ever have imagined.

This is a theme that has played out dozens, even hundreds of times in my life. God prompts me to do something I do not know how to do or don't want to do. I'm reluctant. God nudges me. I obey. And He blesses me with not only the means to achieve what He has asked of me but with successes that I could not have imagined.

When I check in with God first thing in the morning, my day runs efficiently and effectively. I'm in line with God's agenda for me. I offer my energy, my time, my intelligence to advance His Kingdom. Now, this is such a habit that I'm faithful to it. But in the past, when I failed to do this, my day was fated to be off course, wobbly, and inefficient.

### Moving from ordinary to authorized

*And God said, "Let us make man in our image, after our likeness: and let them have dominion over the fish of the sea and over the fowl of the air, and over the cattle, and over the earth, and over every creeping thing that creepeth upon the earth. So God created man in his own image." Genesis 1:26 (KJV)*

In this verse, it is important to note that when God says "let us," by "us," He means the triune God: God the Father, God the Son, and God the Holy Spirit. What's also important to know is that when He talks of making "man" in His image, he is speaking of all humans, not just male humans. In God's creation—unlike my Chinese culture, and unlike so many cultures in the world—men and women are of equal value.

God created the whole world and gave us humans dominion over it. He authorized humans to be in charge of the world He created. When sin is removed, we can reclaim the authority that God offered us to have dominion over it all. We are in a state of constant restoration of this fallen world.

*My people are destroyed for lack of knowledge. Hosea 4:6 (KJV)*

Early in my Christian walk, I did not know that I had such power available to me. I'd been raised to be timid, shy, and meek—the perfect Chinese daughter; the idea of having access to power, much less the supernatural power that God offers to us, was a completely foreign concept. Satan doesn't want us to know we have dominion, authority over disease, sickness, and all of the other matters that face us. If every Christian knew this and exercised their power, Satan would be defeated at every turn.

What God's power in us means is that we can be free from worry of all kinds. I once heard it said that worry is a prayer for what we do not want to happen. My experience is that worry brings great unease, serves no purpose, and is evidence that I have not claimed the rightful power that God has given to me. Rather, we should claim the power with which God endows us, and by doing so, we are freed from worry. Once I learned what "dominion" really meant and that God had given it to all of His children, I knew I had all that I needed to fight the invisible wars we have to fight. We have authority and dominion over all of our circumstances... I didn't know this was spiritual warfare. Once I cast out the spirit of timidity and embraced the power that God has already granted to us all, I did better. I got stronger, braver, and could continue my walk with the Lord without fear.

### God's Word is the truth, and it never changes

*Jesus Christ is the same yesterday, today, and forever. Hebrews 13:8 (KJV)*

It can be difficult from our present-day, earthly existence to look back upon the prophets in the Bible and think of them as "just like us." But indeed, that's exactly what they were. The apostles Matthew, Peter, and Paul, for example, were simple people—Matthew was a tax collector, Peter, a fisherman, Paul started as one of Christianity's most zealous enemies and the other Apostles held equally humble posts. But once they accepted that Jesus Christ was who He said he was, Matthew, Peter, Paul, and the other Apostles were called upon, *authorized*, and commissioned to preach the Gospel and share what they had learned so that others would be saved.

Here's the tricky part: each of us is similarly commissioned, similarly authorized. We are commissioned to preach the Gospel, authorized to do so, and authorized to call upon the Holy Spirit for the supernatural power that is available to all of us. Each of us is given this enormous spiritual authority.

We tend to think of God's miracles as having stopped a few thousand years ago, but that is not at all the case. God's miracles and the powers of the Holy Spirit are equally available to us today as they were to the Apostles of the New Testament.

So you might likely ask how each of us can access the authority that God offers to us. The answer is quite simple: *We invite it and welcome a relationship with God through living in submission to the prompting and downloading of the Holy Spirit. It is our spiritual hearing and seeing.*

From the moment we become born-again Christians, we are endowed with the power and authority to act on God's behalf, even though we may not be aware of it. Seeking His will through prayer and through Bible study is important; it's like daily eating and drinking is to our bodies. Just as we need to nurture our bodies with food and drink every day, we must nurture our spiritual being with prayer and fasting, Bible study, and meditation on God's Holy Word.

Prayer is not simply asking God for things. Prayer creates an attitude of expectancy and communication with God. Again, it is a humble thing to pray. It is recognition of God's power and our surrender to His will for us. We must pray consistently and pray persistently. God does not mind if we "pester" him. In fact, our prayers should be specific. We must give God permission to operate in our lives. This is divine intervention.

I think of prayer as being in a constant state of communication with God. From large issues, like delivering my son from near-death after his car accident, to small things like helping me find a missing necklace, parking space, keys, or glasses, my supplications to God are both an exercise in faith and humility.

Prayer is simply communication with God.

*Do not be anxious about anything, but in every situation, by prayer and petition, with thanksgiving, present your requests to God. And the peace of God, which transcends all understanding, will guard your hearts and your minds in Christ Jesus. Philippians 4:6-77 (NIV)*

It may seem silly to pray about lost glasses or parking spaces, but just imagine how much these small things distract us, cause us stress, and separate us from our sense of peace. Praying always brings an unexplainable peace to us so we are not stressed out over the little things that can set us on a bad path of worry and anxiety.

Recently, Alex, a young seventeen-year-old member of our Bible study group, was facing his SAT tests. Alex is the son of a single mom and does not have much by way of financial support, so he feels a lot of pressure to get into a good school and to make a good living to help support his family as well as his future. Alex came to me and asked me to pray with him to fortify him to take his test. There were special circumstances here too. During the COVID pandemic, because they're being especially cautious, testing opportunities were limited, and Alex would have only one chance to take the test. Before we prayed, Alex told me how anxious he was to take the test because so much rode on his results. You must note that Alex had prepared well and studied hard for this test. He had done his part of the preparation. We prayed together. Following our prayer, Alex reported that he felt at peace and confident in approaching his test day. After he took his test, Alex texted me to report that he had peace throughout the test and that he was confident that he did well. Later, the results would confirm that he had.

God's promise never fails.

*Jesus said, "I also tell you if two of you agree here on earth concerning anything you ask, my Father in heaven will do it for you." Matthew 18:19 (NLT)*

So when Alex and I agreed and prayed together, God fulfilled His promise, the one Jesus spoke about in the above verse. Of course, God always fulfills His promises.

Wait for the Lord;
 be strong and take heart
 and wait for the Lord.

– PSALM 27:14 NIV

**Yes. No. Wait.**

God is not like a Disneyland Daddy, wanting to indulge us to keep us loving Him or buying our affections by granting us our every whim. When we pray to God, we will always get an answer, but, as I've mentioned in an earlier chapter, the answer is not always yes. God answers us in three ways: yes, no, or wait.

God's timing is different from ours. His vision is wider. And He is all-knowing. When God says yes, it is because we are praying for something that is worth honoring and in alignment with His purpose. He knows our motives, and He knows what the outcomes will be. He knows our hearts and our sincerity.

A yes feels wonderful. But sometimes, God answers our prayers with a no. Why? Why would a loving God not give us all that we want? Every parent knows the answer to this question. Sometimes what we want is not what is best for us, and always, our Heavenly Father knows best. When God says no to us, it is not a punishment, as so many think. It is because He knows that what we pray for is not in our best interest. This can be disappointing or even make us angry at God, particularly if we lack the humility and faith to know that God always wants us to be healthy, happy, and well. It's just that what our earthly minds think will make us healthy, happy, and well is minuscule in comparison to what God knows will lead us to be our happiest, healthiest, and best and in His perfect timing, not our own.

Just because God sometimes delays His answers to our prayers, it does not always mean that His answer is no.

**A small adjustment to prayer**

After years of experiencing God's yes/no/wait replies to my prayers, I've learned to pray differently than I once did. Where I might once have asked only for what I wanted, I now honor His wisdom in my prayers. I pray specifically for what I desire, but I always say to God, "I always want your best, rather than my own."

*This foolish plan of God is wiser than the wisest of human plans, and God's weakness is stronger than the greatest of human strength. I Corinthians 1:25 (NLT)*

By adding this humility and respectfulness to our prayer, we honor God, and we make ourselves ready to accept His answer rather than pushing our own agendas. It's a freeing thing to rest in the generous arms of God's will.

It eliminates so much struggle.

Let the peace of Christ rule in your hearts, since as members of one body you were called to peace. And be thankful.
– COLOSSIANS 3:15 NIV

## So what about that chitchat inquiry of God?

Earlier, I mentioned that I like to operate my life in a state of constant chitchat with God. I do not intend here to use such an informal description of prayer to imply that it's a trivial matter. Rather, what I mean by *chitchat* here is that God does not require some special ritual in order to hear our prayers. He can hear us in our vernacular, our casual conversation. It is like talking to our dearest friend, who we know will understand us perfectly.

While the world is full of beautiful churches and extraordinary natural vistas, we do not have to be in a sanctuary or climb to the top of a mountain to pray. If kneeling helps us to be more present and focused for our prayers, that's fine, but God is able to hear us no matter our position or our location. Prayer can be and should be a constant state. As we walk through our day, we can pray. As we cook, play, commute, or work, we can pray.

In a recent Bible study, it came to my attention that Rick Warren teaches that we can do what he calls "popcorn prayer." That's a quick prayer that can be as simple as, "Lord, help!" We have many biblical examples of this from Daniel, David, Peter, and even Jesus, who offer this kind of short prayer. The good news is that no matter how short our prayers may be, God is omniscient. He does not need us to brief Him on the whole story, complete with the background. He already knows it. A simple *popcorn prayer*, even microwave popcorn, is plenty. We can pray for the length of a sentence or dedicate a deeper and more focused time to talk with our Heavenly Father. No appointments necessary.

## An attitude of gratitude

A friend shared a beautiful quote with me:

*To speak gratitude is courteous and pleasant, to enact gratitude is generous and noble, but to live gratitude is to touch heaven.* —Johannes A. Goertner

I have found it to be true that living in gratitude is a big part of walking closely with God. While God is omnipresent—always available to us—it is still true that we should not take God's presence for granted. All this means is that God deserves our praise and our thanks. I've learned that entering my conversations with God through praise, worship, and giving thanks quickly puts me in a prayerful state, making God's presence easier for me to experience. Ultimately prayer is about loving God. There's no specific ritual required. When we are mindful, with an attitude of gratitude, it is never hard to find ways to thank our Heavenly Father.

*Shout with joy to the Lord, all the earth! Worship the Lord with gladness. Come before him, singing with joy. Acknowledge that the Lord is God! He made us, and we are his. We are his people, the sheep of his pasture. Enter his gates with thanksgiving; go into his courts with praise. Give thanks to him and praise his name. For the Lord is good. His unfailing love continues forever, and his faithfulness continues to each generation. Psalms 100:1-5 (NLT)*

## Developing attitudes of gratitude

Gratitude, like so many qualities, is not a set-it-and-forget-it state in our spirits. Gratitude must be welcomed, entertained, and cultivated for it to become a way of life. But gratitude is not meant to be the "product" of receiving God's goodness, but the means by which we experience it.

*In nothing be anxious, but in everything, by prayer and petition with thanksgiving, let your requests be made known to God. And the peace of God, which surpasses all understanding, will guard your hearts and your thoughts in Christ Jesus. Philippians 4:6-7 (WEB)*

In this verse, Apostle Paul says to pray and to petition *with thanksgiving.* It might seem odd to thank God for something in the same breath in which we ask Him for it. But when we think about it more closely, it makes sense. We ask a friend for a favor: *Could you please give me a ride to services next week?* And when that friend agrees to do this, we thank her well in advance of the favor being delivered. We express our gratitude for her simple willingness to honor our request. This is a demonstration of our trust—indeed our faith—in our friend that she will do what she says she will do and an expression of our appreciation for that.

Why then is prayer and petition linked to thanksgiving? Because it is in our thanksgiving, within our prayers of petition, that we express our absolute faith in God.

Many years ago, I faced a huge crisis concerning my daughter's health. I was, as most mothers would be, frantic, desperate, and worried sick. I reached out to a pastor for intercessory healing prayers for my daughter. The pastor's instructions baffled me. She said that I should start my prayers on behalf of my daughter with thanksgiving, praise, and worship.

Now, years later, I begin to understand and experience the wisdom of this pastor's instruction. When we praise and worship God, this brings our spirit to a pinnacle of fellowship and intimacy with God. Praising and thanking Him is an expression of our trust in His goodness and generosity.

I did as my pastor instructed. I praised and worshiped God in my supplication for my daughter. This act of faith encouraged me, deepening my faith. Even in the middle of this crisis, singing praise, giving thanks, and worshiping reminded me of the power and greatness of God.

Prior to this event, it had never occurred to me that thanksgiving, praise, and worship are all in the same package with prayer and petition. Of course, it is much easier to praise and offer thanksgiving to God when all is well and when sailing is smooth. It was not easy—at least at first—to praise God in the midst of my fear and worry about my daughter's severe health issue. But throughout that period, I had the beginnings of a revelation that would change my relationship with prayer for my lifetime. The revelation is both simple and profound: ***Praise is a sacrifice.***

*Therefore, let us offer through Jesus a continual sacrifice of praise to God, proclaiming our allegiance to his name. And don't forget to do good and to share with those in need. These are the sacrifices that please God. Hebrews 13:15-16 (NLT)*

Prayer and petition are—or should be—a part of every Christian's everyday lifestyle. So too, should be thanksgiving, praise, and worship. Of course, I remain in the process of growing in faith, always learning to embrace this "attitude of gratitude" at deeper and deeper levels. But I'll also say that today, gratitude to God is much easier for me than it once was. Throughout the decades, my life has not been without hardship, heartbreak, and loss. And still, through all of that, God has demonstrated His goodness, generosity, and power in all circumstances. Through this, my faith has grown. Gratitude, praise, and worship are much more of an instinct for me now, where once there would have been worry and doubt.

Many are very familiar with the following two verses. But I invite you to look at them more closely to really know what the psalmist is trying to tell us about what pleases God.

*But you are holy, enthroned in the praise of Israel\*. Psalm 22:3 (NKJV)*

**(\*Meaning all of us.)**

*Enter his gates with thanksgiving; go into his courts with praise. Give thanks to him and praise his name. For the Lord is good. Psalm 100:4-5a (NLT)*

When I practice thanksgiving, praising, and worshiping God, I find it so much easier to enter into his presence... to feel intimately connected with Him. These acts are deeply powerful because they bring the presence and anointing of God into our midst. Many faith services today begin with songs of worship, praise, and thanksgiving. Note that this is *at the beginning* of the service, bringing God into an intimate connection with us.

When God comes into the scene, sickness is healed, lack is filled to overflowing, sadness turns to joy, worry turns to hope, turmoil turns to peace. This is immensely powerful to know and an invaluable tool in our daily walk in faith. Each of us can bring down heaven where all of the riches of God dwell.

The following short video is of a physical manifestation of God's presence during worship and praise. The parishioners of Bethel Church were praising God with deep fervor, and God blessed them. Of course, skeptics have rightfully questioned this event. But in a moment, I'll share a similar experience that I witnessed with my own eyes, which makes me more trusting of this video.

Take a look at "Glory Cloud at Bethel Church": http://youtu.be/lvJMPccZR2Y.

Let me offer a personal story of God manifesting in a physical way. Many years ago, I hosted a Christian Ladies' lunch for Peggy Cole, the prophetess, at the St. Francis Yacht Club in San Francisco. As we were singing hymns of praise at dessert time, suddenly, gold dust began to appear on many of our palms. It was not smeared all over the tables. No one had sprinkled glitter on our dessert plates. The glistening dust simply appeared on our palms. Peggy Cole had the most amount of dust on both of her palms. I, too, had some, though not as much as her. Just as in the video I shared above, God demonstrated His presence in a physical way during a time of praise, worship, and thanksgiving. This is a supernatural phenomenon that I will never forget. The glory of the Lord appeared right before us!

Thanksgiving is an equally, if not more, important and powerful part of our prayer and petition as it demonstrates our uncompromised faith in His omniscience, omnipotence, and omnipresence. It demonstrates that we believe in His immutable love and the salvation that He has offered.

Thanksgiving, praise, and worship are not only a

demonstration of our faith but also serve to increase our faith in God's goodness. It is not by accident that I named this book *God is Good.* Even the title I chose is a demonstration of living with an attitude of gratitude, as well as a statement of the importance of praise as an element of faith in what God has already prepared and accomplished for us.

Gratitude to God does not say that "nothing bad is going on." Satan, enemies, sickness, adverse circumstances, and all negative things not of God are out of our sight in the midst of praise and thanksgiving. Light replaces darkness. Good eclipses evil. Trust subjugates doubt. Hope shines over despair.

Praise and thanksgiving are among our most invaluable tools when it comes to spiritual warfare. We cannot win the victory in advancing God's Kingdom if we do not practice praise and thanksgiving. This is why it so displeases God when we do not have faith in Him. After all, He deserves it.

*Without faith, it is impossible to please God. Hebrews 11:6 (NIV)*

The value of praise, worship, and thanksgiving deserve deep contemplation and study. The Scriptures are full of examples of those who had an "attitude of gratitude," as well as the stories that demonstrate the blessings of this way of living. Below are some vivid examples:

1.Praise enabled Abraham, at age 100, to stay in faith and to receive God's promise of a son, Isaac.

*But Abraham never doubted... he praised God for this blessing even before it happened. He was completely sure that God was able to do anything He promised. Romans 4:20-21 (LB)*

For Abraham and Sarah to have a son at ages 100 and 90 is a medical impossibility, of course. Abraham's secret was to stay in faith, and he never wavered in his praise and thanks to God. He praised God for the blessing long before it happened. This praise brought about a miracle. This is a perfect example of thanking God in advance for receiving His promise.

2. Corporate praise and worship win spiritual warfare.

The Israelites took down the walls of Jericho—something that today could only be achieved with bulldozers—and won the battle without a fight. The battle was won because they followed God's instructions. God told them to march around the city for six days and on the seventh day to sing praises.

I ask you here to imagine this carefully. This is an army prepared to fight. And they obeyed God by simply marching for six days, and rather than fighting on the seventh, they sang their praise to God. What kind of faith would that require?

*Now the gates of Jericho were tightly shut because the people were afraid of the Israelites. No one was allowed to go out or in. But the Lord said to Joshua, 'I have given you Jericho, its king, and all its strong warriors. You and your fighting men should march around the town once a day for six days. Seven priests will walk ahead of the Ark, each carrying a ram's horn. On the seventh day you are to march around the town seven times, with the priests blowing the horns. When you hear the priests give one long blast on the rams' horns, have all of the people shout as loud as they can. Then the walls of the town will collapse, and the people can charge straight into the town. Joshua 6:1-5 (NLT)*

The Israelites did exactly as God instructed, and when they did, God fulfilled His promise: the walls fell down. They did not fight with weapons made of steel or clubs made of wood in this battle. They obeyed God, praised Him *before* He answered their prayers, and God gave them victory. Praise and worship are spiritual weapons to defeat Satan, our enemy.

Have you ever felt worried and anxious while listening to the news? When spiritual Jerichos (panic attacks, worry, anxiety, fearfulness, and negative emotions) begin to engulf us, the instruction God offers in the story of Jericho is that we can employ today. When the worry takes over, do a counterattack immediately with worship, thanksgiving, and praise. You'll be surprised at how the walls of fear and anxiety crumble, just as they did at Jericho. The fears will dissipate. The worry will pass. Praise will fill you with hope and faith.

3. Praise prepares the way for God's supernatural intervention.

*But giving thanks is a sacrifice that truly honors me. If you keep to my path, I will reveal to you the salvation of God. Psalm 50:23 (NLT)*

*It's the praising life that honors me. As soon as you set your foot on the Way, I'll show you my salvation. Psalm 50:23 (MSG)*

In our weekly ladies group fellowship, we prayed with thanksgiving for a sister going through a most devastating divorce. Her ex-husband had ceased giving support for their seven-year-old son. In addition, he was also trying to take everything from her. Of course, I understood this pain and worry, as I remembered my own divorce from Ex many years before. But because we prayed with thanksgiving, many miracles came to pass. They may seem simple by comparison to the crumbling walls of Jericho, but God cares about our smallest concerns as well as the large battles in the world.

In one instance, right after we prayed with much praise and gratitude, our prayer group member experienced such a miracle. She had a luxury car that had always been in her husband's name. She herself had presented the pink slip to the DMV. But when she went to the DMV again, trying to transfer the title to her name, somehow this had already been done. The vehicle was registered in her own name, though she knew that neither she nor her ex had changed it. This prayer was answered within half an hour of our prayers of thanksgiving. As I always say, God IS good, and He works in unseen and mysterious ways... even through the DMV.

4.Jesus gave thanks first, then fed 5000 with two small fish and five loaves of bread.

Many are familiar with the story of Jesus feeding the masses with only two small fish and five loaves of bread. Of course, this is a miracle that demonstrates God's compassion and abundance. However, in the context I write about here, there's another aspect of this miracle to be explored. Before God multiplied the loaves and fish, Jesus praised Him. It was this praise that brought forth God's abundance.

*And he directed the people to sit down on the grass. Taking the five loaves and the two fish and looking up to heaven, he gave thanks... Matthew 14:19 (NIV)*

5.In the Lord's Prayer, Jesus gave honor and glory at the beginning and at the ending of the prayer.

Again, the words of the Lord's Prayer may be highly familiar, but I invite you to look at them more closely. Here, I've included the first and last lines of this familiar prayer. It serves as a model for praying with an attitude of praise and thanksgiving.

*"Our father which art in heaven, hallowed be thy name. Thy kingdom come, thy will be done in earth, as it is in heaven... For thine is the kingdom, and power, and glory forever, Amen." Matthew 6:11-13 (KJV)*

6.Jesus gave thanks to the Father and resurrected Lazarus from the dead.

*Father, thank you for hearing me. John 11: 41b (NLT)*

*Then Jesus shouted, "Lazarus, come out!" And the dead man came out." John 11:43-44a (NLT)*

From the Old Testament to the New Testament, from the very lips of our Savior, from a ladies' prayer group to a luncheon at a yacht club, praise and thanksgiving are the tools to appropriate everything in the unseen spiritual world. The battles over suffering, sickness, disease, poverty and worry have already been won. When we know this, *deeply* know it, it is easy to give thanks at the beginning and end of our every prayer.

*All praise be to God, the Father of our Lord Jesus Christ, who has blessed us with every spiritual blessing in the heavenly realms because we are united with Christ. Even before he made the world, God loved us and chose us in Christ to be holy and without fault in his eyes God decided in advance to adopt us into his own family by bringing us to himself through Jesus Christ. This is what he wanted to do, and it gave him great pleasure. So we praise God for the glorious grace he has poured out on us who belong to his dear Son. He is so rich in kindness and grace that he purchased our freedom with the blood of his Son and forgave our sins. He has showered his kindness on us, along with all wisdom and understanding. Ephesians 1:3-8 (NLT)*

Hallelujah. Hallelujah! *HALLELUJAH!*

**Abundance is yours**

I often hear people question why God has not answered their prayers. If they have had long struggles with finances or health and feel as though they have prayed, it can feel as though God has either not answered or has answered with "no."

It is crucial to remember that God wants abundance

for all of His children. Even if you've struggled with a condition of deprivation for a long time, you must know that God wants you to have plenty; He wants your needs filled. He wants you to live in abundance, not with the leftovers or scraps of the world, but its riches.

Reverend Jentezen Franklin offers a fascinating sermon on this topic, titled *God Wants to Prosper You.* (YouTube, "God Wants to Prosper You," https://youtu. be/_5GOSXV4uJo (5/31/16) Franklin cites the importance of believing in God's abundance in order to experience God's abundance. He contends that the Scriptures tell us about God's wish for us to live in abundance and joy.

*"Let them shout for joy and be glad who favor my righteous cause; And let them say continually, "Let the lord be magnified, who has pleasure in the prosperity of His servant." (Psalm 35:27 NKJV)*

So many people think of having a relationship with God as being only a pious and serious practice. But notice here that God wants his children to "shout for joy and be glad." God delights when we honor what He provides for us, act as good stewards, and grow what He's given us into a life of plenty.

**But really, what is prayer anyway? Can't God just read our minds?**

Yes, God can read our minds. He is omniscient. But He gave us free will. He needs our permission to intervene in our lives. Simply put, prayer is an intimate conversation with God. Not just talking, but listening as well. God, our heavenly Father, loves us, His children. He wishes to talk with us.

It was not until I hit a crisis in my first marriage that I experienced the importance of talking to our Heavenly Father sincerely and earnestly. Prior to this crisis, I just sort of prayed the Lord's Prayer here and there. I didn't really know how to talk to God. In my utter desperation, I had the most heart-wrenching and sincere talk with God. To my great shock and surprise, He answered my prayer in two weeks. As I said earlier, this is when my then-husband decided to file for divorce, something he had been dead set against until that time.

Prior to this time, my prayer life was hit or miss. Sometimes I prayed; sometimes, I did not. And even when I did pray, I was never sure God heard me. I didn't understand why it seemed that sometimes my prayers were answered, and other times they seemed ignored.

Yes, I know the verses well:

*Keep on asking, and you will receive what you ask for. Keep on seeking, and you will find. Keep on knocking, and the door will be opened to you. For everyone who asks, receives. Everyone who seeks, finds. And to everyone who knocks, the door will be opened. Matthew 7:7-8 (NLT)*

But even though I knew these verses, I did not feel as though I received the answers to my prayers as they described. I came to realize that my prayers were too general; I needed to pray with specificity. So when I prayed specifically for the sum of $100K to provide for my children's future college education, God answered beyond my wildest expectations.

*Yet you don't have what you want because you don't ask God for it, James 4:2b (NLT)*

You see, God is a gentleman, not a big boss. He gives us free will to lead our lives as we choose. If we do not ask Him, He will not force His will upon us. This verse is very clear and simple; we have to ask. We have to invite Him to intervene in our lives.

Just try it—God is good.

*Don't worry about anything; instead pray about everything. Tell God what you need and thank him for all he has done. Then you will experience God's peace, which exceeds anything we can understand. His peace will guard your hearts and minds as you live in Jesus Christ. Philippians 4:6-7 (NLT)*

When God answered my prayers about my first marriage, and when He again answered them to provide for my children, I began to see the light. I worried because I did not pray about everything that I was worried about. So I started, just a little at a time, to pray about things, people, situations, and circumstances that gave me worry. I tried it… and God answered my prayers! I experienced indescribable peace. I became deeply fond of the peace that exceeded my understanding and welcomed it as a beautiful replacement for my worry and anxiety. His peace is in my heart and in my mind. Praise the Lord. This is how I began my prayer life—an intimate relationship with God. I found out that God loves to talk to me. He is talking to me all the time. I learned that I could talk to him *before* I mess up, seeking His divine guidance, rather than doing everything on my own and having to pray HELP! I can seek His best advice and will for me, for my family and friends. I do not have to settle for what I thought was best, which is far less than the beautiful life that God wants for all of His children.

God has a perfect plan for each and every one of us. Like all earthly parents, our Heavenly Father wants to grant us His very best. Today, I urge you to start, resume, continue, or deepen your conversation with God. He is there to hear your concerns. He can and will provide all that you need because He is our inexhaustible supply. Our heavenly Father is the creator of heaven and earth. He spoke into being the sun, moon, stars, and every seed-bearing plant and tree, every bird, fish, and animal big and small. He spoke humans into being. He created us to share His abundance with us.

The Apostle Paul admonishes us on prayer with thanksgiving in his letter to the saints in Thessalonia.

*Always be joyful. Never stop praying. Be thankful in all circumstances, for this is God's will for you who belong to Christ Jesus. I Thessalonians 5:16-18 (NLT)*

On the subject of prayer, I am learning every day. As you continue in developing your own prayer life, I highly recommend two books by Kenneth E. Hagin: *Art of Prayer: Steps to Answered Prayer* and *Will of God in Prayer*.

*Then God said, "Let Us (Father, Son, Holy Spirit) make man in Our image, according to Our likeness [not physical, but a spiritual personality and moral likeness]; and let them have complete authority over the fish of the sea, the birds of he air, the cattle, and over the entire earth, and over everything that creeps and crawls on the earth" So God created man in His own image, in the image and likeness of God He created him: male and female He created them. Genesis 1:26-27 (AMP)*

This passage tells us of another kind of prayer. One kind of prayer is about petitioning God, asking for His help and guidance. But here, we see also that God instructed Adam and Eve to exercise their authority… to "command" with authority. This is best exemplified when we are asking for healing. Rather than simply asking God to heal us of a physical or emotional illness, we are to claim spiritual authority and *command in the name of Jesus* for that illness to leave us.

Let me bring this idea a little more down to earth. A traffic policeman, standing in the middle of the road directing traffic, has authority. He is small, standing in an intersection when a huge truck comes toward him. But he's been "authorized" by the uniform and badge that he wears. He must merely raise his hand to the truck driver to make the huge vehicle come to a stop. This is the kind of authority that we have been given by God.

The things we face might feel huge: like the wildfires we are facing in California as I write this, like hurricanes along the Gulf Coast, and the novel coronavirus pandemic that has had an impact throughout the world, or even something personal like cancer in the body of a loved one. Like that truck approaching the intersection, we can feel so small against forces so huge. And we, as born-again Christians, are told that we have authority, dominion over all that is on Earth. So it can be confusing to us—even to those of us who are mature in our faith—to understand why when we command rain to come to ease the wildfires, or we command cancer to leave the body of someone we love, that the difficulty is not always instantly remedied.

I cannot pretend to understand all things. I cannot pretend to understand why sometimes when I exercise authority in the name of Jesus that the effect is immediate, and other times it is not. But remember, God answers yes/no/ maybe. And He sees best. It is faith in this that strengthens us, and it is our faith that honors God and for which He honors us in return.

Prayer can be our beautiful invitation to God, asking Him to intervene, provide, guide, and support us. Our prayers are best when they are sincere. They are most easily heard when we are living righteously, without the presence of sin that separates us from God. And when we send up such beautiful invitations, God always RSVPs.

*The heartfelt and persistent prayer of a righteous man (believer) is able to accomplish much [when put into action and made effective by god—it is dynamic and can have tremendous power.] James 5:16 (AMP)*

In this verse, I am reminded that the kind of person we are will affect the outcome of our prayers. The more righteously we live in God's sight, the more God will answer our prayers with a yes. This is because when you are living in line with God, you will not pray for things that are against His will.

## My personal "burning bush" story

Prayer, simply stated, is communication with God. In the Bible, God spoke to Moses by appearing as a burning bush that did not get consumed by the fire. This says to us that God's voice is everlasting and will never be vanquished. Sometimes it seems that people wait for grand images like a burning bush as evidence of God's voice. But often, God speaks to us in simple, less theatrical ways. Sometimes He speaks by putting an opportunity or a resource before us or sending a special person or a sermon from a skilled minister to inspire us. Sometimes—and in my experience, as often as we ask of Him—He simply speaks to us.

Our job is to listen.

A lot of people think of prayer as a one-sided experience with us talking to God; this is not true at all. The most important aspect of prayer is not what WE say to God but listening to His voice. I've heard it said that because we are given two ears and one mouth that we should use them in that proportion. It has taken me some time in my walk with God, but I have learned to listen for His voice as a predominant part of my own prayer life.

As I've shared, it is my habit to wake early in the morning to talk to God and to commit the day to Him. Each day I thank Him for another day to experience His goodness. Every day is a rich and precious gift from God with new grace and new opportunities.

*This is the day that the Lord has made; we will rejoice and be glad in it. Psalm 118:24 (KJV)*

In October of 2004, my husband, Ted, and I were living quite happily in a San Francisco condominium in the Nob Hill neighborhood. It was a fine home, and we had no intention of moving, thinking we had the home we could stay in for the remainder of our days.

Our upstairs neighbor had a leak from their refrigerator that flowed down to our residence. This caused great damage to our apartment and necessitated us staying elsewhere during the repairs. We initially thought this would be about one month, but, as such things often do, it turned out that it would take over three months. We were fortunate to find a rental available in a highly desirable building in downtown San Francisco. There were units for sale in that building, and the facilities and services offered there were pleasing, but we were not even entertaining the idea of moving as we'd been perfectly content in our other home. We were gratefully living in a beautiful home, seeking nothing more.

One morning that October, I woke up at 4 a.m., my usual time of prayer and worship. I was surprised when God spoke clearly to me, saying, "Margaret, go and make an offer on apartment 31-A today." His voice was clear and specific, and He was urging me to invest in a home in that new building.

I woke Ted up and told him the message. He murmured his okay and told me to call our personal broker, George Ju. Then he rolled over and went back to sleep.

Because George Ju was in China at the time, I thought that I'd just wait until he returned. But God spoke to me again, just as clearly. "May I remind you that you were a broker, and your husband is a lawyer. Call the listing broker and ask her to bring a contract so the two of you can get this done." Though I'd long ago retired from my real estate career, God was still making use of what He'd provided me so long ago.

By this time in my Christian walk, I had learned not to disregard God's urgings, so I called the listing broker, Janet Krahling, right away, asking her to bring a contract over. She suggested that I should not even bother because she was already presenting two offers to the sellers at 9 a.m. Well, I had no desire to get into a bidding war, so I thought that was it. But no. God spoke again. "Margaret, make an offer today."

This, you must take note, was not coming from my own desire. That's part of how I knew it was God's prompting. I had no longing to buy a new home. What's more, was that I didn't want to have a complicated and expensive bidding war. I didn't want to do the expensive and time-consuming tasks of preparing our home to sell it. I had no lust for a home finer or more luxurious than we had. The timing was bad for us because we were going to be going on a cruise to Sydney, Australia, in January, and our own home was still undergoing repairs. But God was insistent.

Because of God's insistence, despite Janet's discouragement, I asked her to bring a contract. Ted and I offered a bid below the asking price. Now it's important to know that in a bidding war, prices usually exceed asking, so we did not believe that we would be successful with our bid. But, as I've said before, when God wants us to do something, and we obey, He clears the way for it to happen. It should be of no surprise (because this whole endeavor was prompted by God in the first place) that our offer was accepted.

But then, of course, we had another problem: selling the home we had. And again, God provided. We interviewed brokers and found an excellent one in Joel Goodrich. We let him know that we had already bought a new home, so we were anxious to sell quickly and that we'd be out of the country during any transaction. All of this seemed impossible!

On the second day of our cruise, Joel called. We'd received an offer on the first day of the listing, significantly above our asking price. This was far above our wildest expectations.

Ted likes to say that I saw a burning bush in our bedroom at 4 a.m. that October morning. He likes to say that God appeared to me but that he saw no burning bush at all. But I tell the story as an example of God's voice both nudging me toward a wise investment and clearing all obstacles so that it could happen.

There are a few lessons in this "burning bush" story. Of course, it is a story about listening to God, recognizing

His voice, and heeding his urgings.

*Oh, taste and see that the Lord is good; Blessed is the man who trusts Him! Oh fear the Lord, you His saints! There is no want to those who fear Him. Psalms 34:8-9 (NKJV)*

This story is also a lesson about God's desire for us to prosper. Ted and I did not seek more luxury or a larger home. But since we have lived in this place—much larger than we thought we'd need—it has been a place that I've been able to use for God's glory. I host Bible study and fundraising events there. It's a comfortable home that serves Ted and me well as we age. It is a good investment that has appreciated in value, allowing us to prosper further and to use that money in the service of the Lord. It is home.

Earlier, in November of 1999, God guided Ted and me to purchase another property. God would guide us to invest in a home north of San Francisco in the Sonoma Valley, which is Wine Country. It's a beautiful place and provides Ted and me a splendid retreat and a place to host our grandchildren. But again, we did not seek this as a luxury but were prompted by God to invest wisely in it. Following God's prompting in investments and purchases is part of being a good steward.

*I said to the Lord, "You are my Master! Every good thing I have comes from you." Psalm 16:2 (NLT)*

Praise the LORD, O my soul, and forget not all his benefits-
—Psalm 103:2 Niv

## Speaking in the language of angels

I've addressed the maturing of my own faith and the way in which my prayer life has evolved over time, making prayer a more constant state rather than seeing it as a special occasion. There exists another level of conversation with God that has changed my life in ways I could not possibly have imagined. It has allowed me, more than nearly anything else, to access the supernatural authority that God makes available to all of us.

Through the Holy Spirit, the gift of speaking in tongues is the means by which we can bypass the limits of our human understanding. Don't let the language concern you. The word "tongues" when we talk of speaking in tongues when translated from Greek simply means "language." Speaking in tongues is simply speaking in a heavenly language. This is also known as The Baptism of the Holy Spirit.

This is how the disciples of Jesus first experienced this particular gift of the Holy Spirit:

*When the day of Pentecost came, they were all together in one place. Suddenly a sound like the blowing of a violent wind came from heaven and filled the whole house where they were sitting. They saw what seemed to be tongues of fire that separated and came to rest on each of them. All of them were filled with the Holy Spirit and began to speak in other tongues as the Spirit enabled them. Acts 2:1-4 (NIV)*

Speaking in unknown tongues can sound intimidating and mysterious to many. In our "natural" world, such supernatural experiences can seem strange. But God Himself is supernatural, meaning He is simply *beyond natural*—"natural" in terms of this world. The Holy Spirit's gift of speaking in tongues is quite natural in the spiritual realm and is offered to us all.

My own experience with praying in tongues is that it is a powerful way to pray straight to the throne room of

God. It is a prayer initiated by the Holy Spirit that gives utterance to my spirit.

While God can understand our most casual speech, and it is good to access Him through this means, our earthly language, or mother tongue, remains just that—earthly. God understands it, of course, but the hazard of our earthly languages is that our mind, where language lives, can be a place of vulnerability. When using familiar words, it is easy for us to rely on our intellect in our conversations with God. We can try to talk God into or out of things. We can press for our own agendas. We can even limit our prayers to a finite reality rather than accessing the infinite possibilities that exist through God.

### *Speaking in tongues is a "perfect prayer" in God's view*

Faith does not reside in our minds; faith resides in our spirits. So, doesn't it make sense that we should have access to a spiritual language with which to talk to God? And doesn't it also make sense that God's voice would be clearer to us when we have bypassed our human language and have tapped into a spiritual one? It is the Holy Spirit speaking to and through my spirit.

That is exactly what my introduction to speaking of tongues was: my spiritual, supernatural (beyond natural) experience of God.

### My Baptism of the Holy Spirit

In 1992, I had been struggling with worry for my son, my daughter, my father who was suffering prostate cancer at the time, and other concerns for my earthly existence. In short, I was stressed out. I attended a conference led by Kenneth E. Hagin, held at Hilton Hotel in San Francisco. This was a conference dedicated to pursuing the supernatural powers of God through the healing gifts of the Holy Spirit, and I knew that God wanted me at this particular conference.

At one point during a break at the conference, I was introduced to few other participants who I'd been told had the gift of "activating" others to speak in tongues. One of these people was a kind man and devout Christian named John Harrison who has the fascinating—and what many might consider an enviable—job and gift. He's been long described as the "man with the million-dollar taste buds." John was then the official ice cream taste-tester for Dreyer's Ice Cream company, and he used his highly sensitive palate to discern and develop new ice cream flavors. He gained his moniker because Dreyer's found his skills so valuable that they insured his taste buds for one million dollars. And while John's job may sound, well, delicious, I came to appreciate from him a much more important gift. Not only was John then able to speak in tongues, but he was also skilled at activating others to do so as well. I had no idea how important this would become in my life as a Christian.

John Harrison and two others—each people of powerful faith—laid hands on me as they prayed in tongues. To my earthly ears, this might've sounded like gibberish, but an undeniable and profound transformation occurred.

*If any man thirsts, let him come unto me and drink. He that believeth on me, as the scripture hath said, out of his belly shall flow rivers of living water. John 7:37b-38 (KJV)*

During that prayer, an overwhelming vision came to me. God gave me a glimpse into the angelic realm. I saw—literally *saw* (not imagined, dreamed, or hoped to see)—seven angels surrounding me, each huge, more than seven feet tall. They were locking their wings, forming a protective circle around me. During this vision, while the prayers swirled around me and the angels held their protective circle, I saw my body lifted up to one foot above the ground. Yes, I felt myself levitate and began to speak in tongues myself, with a ferocious velocity that I, on my own, could never have manufactured. It was clear that this language, what to some would sound like gibberish, was supernatural—above and beyond the natural world. This was an angelic visitation.

I was deeply and profoundly surprised by this vision as it was beyond anything I'd ever experienced. During this vision, God's voice was clear. He said, "I'm showing you this vision so that you know you don't need to be stressed out. I send angels to protect you, to guide you, to go to war for you. You are on this earth, but you are above this world."

I'm even hesitant to write about this event for fear that it sounds like fiction, or a fantasy, or even a delusion. But I know in my heart what was real, and I trust that God will honor my telling it and that it will serve those who read it. I must be faithful to God's vision, and I know that He would not have provided this vision if He didn't want me to share it. And because the experience of speaking in tongues has proven to be such an invaluable and powerful part of my relationship with God, I feel I must share it here.

By bypassing my earthly mind, my intellect, by the use of speaking in tongues, I was able to circumvent the earthly logic of my finite mind that would talk me out of this supernatural experience. And still, God used the senses of my body to communicate; He offered sights, sounds, and sensations in my body that I could understand in order to communicate beyond my understanding.

This life-changing experience deepened and broadened my faith and made my conversations with God that much more intimate. It has allowed me to see into the angelic realm.

Learning to speak in tongues is like having a close friend born in a different country than your own who speaks a language in which you have an extremely limited vocabulary. You struggle to speak clearly because you love this friend, but you have to patch together fragments and phrases to get the meaning of the conversation. Even when you do this with love and a great desire to articulate your deepest and most sincere thoughts, the limits of your language keep you from the fluency with which you wish you could communicate. Imagine if you suddenly woke up one day fluent in your dear friend's language, and you instantly have a deeper understanding of all that he's trying to tell you. What was once a patched-together bit of conversation becomes a fluent, limitless exchange of meaning, understanding, and intimacy.

Our finite minds are limited to what we understand. Speaking in tongues is simply a more efficient and effective way to pray. When we pray in this supernatural way, we bring in God's perfect will, not our human perception of how things should be. To welcome this gift is to elevate our level of prayer.

*The prayers of a righteous person are powerful and effective. James 5:16 (KJV)*

John Harrison's earthly gift was quantifiable as one million dollars by an insurance company. His gifts have helped Dreyer's to become a successful ice cream business. But the earthly value of his valuable taste buds is minuscule compared to the value he offers to advance God's kingdom because he uses his spiritual gifts to activate others to theirs.

Through speaking in tongues, I now know how to access God's heavenly wishes, not just the earthly ones. I've learned a great deal from John Harrison and have discovered that I too can activate others and have used my own gifts to help bring others to accept Christ.

Our earthly lives maybe, if we are very fortunate, one hundred years long. All of the treasures and pleasures we acquire here can be enjoyed only for that duration. But when we build spiritual treasures, those last for eternity. On earth, I am a woman of wealth. But that wealth pales in comparison to my riches in heaven.

When we measure eternal gifts against whatever rewards we might enjoy in our hundred years on earth, it's easy to give up temporary pleasures for the sake of the treasures we will enjoy when we are spending eternity with our Heavenly Father.

And I'm sure that John Harrison would agree that eternity with God is even better than an endless supply of ice cream.

## Welcoming this gift of the Holy Spirit

In his lesson called "Overcoming Hindrances to Speaking in Tongues" (YouTube, https://youtu.be/ZLIx_cecYs4, March 12, 2012), Russell Walden describes speaking in tongues this way:

*"Speaking in tongues is a grace and a gift. It brings great power and deploys and activates the powers and strength of God in your life."*

What Pastor Walden describes here is exactly my experience. I was a faithful Christian for many years, striving to walk closely with God. But it was when I embraced the supernatural power—remember this only means beyond natural—of speaking with God in this unencumbered way that I was able to experience the true power of God in my life and to find the solutions to my earthly problems and difficulties in a heavenly realm. Walden says something profound that drives this home:

*"You can't solve a problem on the level of the problem."*

In other words, we cannot solve earthly difficulties with earthly solutions in earthly language. We must rise above our level and use what Walden describes as "God speak" (aka, speaking in tongues). We rise from the natural world to the realm of angels to solve our earthly problems.

Speaking in tongues is also called Baptism of the Holy Spirit. It is one of the spiritual gifts and one that I was surprised to learn how truly powerful it is. When we pray in tongues, we are circumventing our limited human minds, and as Walden describes it, we are "speaking in the realm of angels" in a way that "circumvents our objections, doubts, and controversies of the mind."

## Taking the strangeness out of the supernatural

For many, the idea of speaking in tongues is peculiar. And, admittedly, by our earthly standards, it is! But again, we're not talking about earthly language; we're talking about heavenly language. What's more, to speak in tongues is not a gift just given to some; it is a capability that we already have inside of us, even if we've not ever tried it.

Further in Walden's talk, he explains that when we are born in our earthly bodies, but for those born with profound disabilities, we are all born with the capacity for language. Babies babble and coo, their parents and caretakers nurture their gibberish into understandable language. And while it took a bit of learning to develop fluency, we already had the capability for language when we were born.

When we are born again, by accepting Jesus, we are also born with the capacity to speak in this heavenly language; we just need to welcome it into our spirits, not only into our minds. There's a bit of a battle to be fought here. You see, our minds are possessive. They do not want to surrender our language centers, but when we surrender, our minds, our spirits, and our spiritual language can take over. But know this: you already have the capacity to accept this gift of the Holy Spirit.

But why speak in tongues, you might ask? Can't God understand English or Cantonese or Spanish? Of course, He can understand us, whatever language we speak. But when we are using language that we understand, we are subject to the vulnerabilities and limitations of our minds.

And we need not fear speaking in tongues. It's not like a magic spell that is cast upon us. No, it is a gift that is given, and we welcome it voluntarily with cooperation and consent.

### Speaking in tongues for spiritual fitness

*For if you have the ability to speak in tongues, or in unknown languages; you will be talking only to God, since people won't be able to understand you. You will be speaking by the power of the Spirit, or speaking in your spirit, but it will all be mysterious. I Corinthians 14:2 (NLT)*

The most important aspect of speaking in tongues is it

edifies ourselves and strengthens our spirit. Just as physical exercise strengthens our muscles, speaking in tongues exercises our spiritual selves. When we pray in tongues, most of the time, we do know what we are praying. That's okay. That's why most people stop praying in tongues, thinking there's no reason to pray without understanding. But our natural mind cannot comprehend the things of God.

There are many things for which we must pray without understanding them. That's where the Holy Spirit and speaking in tongues comes in. I stopped speaking in tongues for twenty years. During that period of time, I brought very few people to the Lord through my testimony. Preaching the gospel is not done by might but by the power of the Holy Spirit. In 2012, I decided to speak in tongues again. It was brought about by Peggy Cole, who "reactivated" me.

As a result, I have been able to bring many people to the Lord, even those with whom I have a brief or casual contact: business colleagues, taxi drivers, waiters, and sales clerks. I have been able to activate people, just like that. And many have come to the Lord because of this experience.

Subsequently, I have learned that I can ask for the Holy Spirit to give me an interpretation of my prayers. Mind you, this is an interpretation, not a verbatim translation of tongues to English. Nowadays, when my prayer group gathers to pray to intercede for others, we start by praying with our minds in understanding. And we finish by praying together in tongues. The results are always amazing, truly above and beyond what any of us could have imagined.

**Not just for God's understanding**

*And these signs will follow those who believe…they will speak with new tongues. Mark 16:17 (KJV)*

Robert Morris ("Does He Speak in Tongues?" YouTube 10/28/2020, https://www.youtube.com/watch?v=omJ64X-uEnMo&f eature=youtu.be) calls the speaking in tongues "speaking in purity." This purity honors God.

When we speak in tongues in our prayers, it is not simply for God's benefit, though He is honored by our prayers. He understands whatever language we speak, of course. By speaking in tongues, what we are doing is leaping over earthly, human barriers to understand the mystery of God. *What we access is God's omniscience.*

Yes. I really do mean that. God wants us to know and see and understand in the supernatural realm, unbound by earthly limitations. He is not stingy with His wisdom; He wants it for us all.

By speaking in tongues and welcoming all of the gifts of the Holy Spirit, we all—every single person of faith—have a backstage pass to God's greatness. Our faith becomes supercharged because it becomes limitless.

### The Triune God—three equal parts

*And we all, who with unveiled faces contemplate the Lord's Glory, are being transformed into His image with ever-increasing glory, which comes from the Lord, who is the Spirit. II Corinthians 3:18 (NIV)*

It is important to note that when it comes to the influence of the Triune God—the Father, Son, and Holy Spirit— nobody gets second billing. There is no competition between the three for a starring role. The three aspects of God are each of equal importance, working with equal mystery, magnificence, and power. While it's easier for some to envision a creator and a savior, it is sometimes challenging for us to imagine the vastness and power of the Holy Spirit and to value His role in our spiritual walk.

In her article "What is the Holy Spirit and 10 Supernatural Ways He Empowers You," (https://www.crosswalk.com/faith/spiritual-life/10-supernatural-ways-the-holy-spirit-wants-to-empower-you.html), Brittany Rust succinctly describes not only what the Holy Spirit is but also how we can welcome His influence in our everyday lives.

Rust describes the Holy Spirit and His many functions

with clarity. Essentially, she describes the following roles of the Holy Spirit:

- As our helper, when we are feeling powerless or afraid

- To sanctify or "purify" us, helping us to grow more Christ-like

- To help us to do God's will

- To empower our ministry to others

- To make us feel loved by God

- To give us hope in hopeless times

- To give us deeper insight into God's ways

- To guide our prayers beyond our own understanding

This is not the role of a minor player in God's Kingdom! This, just as is true for God the Father and Jesus, is equally important, a starring role, if you will.

**Brain science and speaking in tongues**

When people first hear about the gift of speaking in tongues, they often think it seems like mumbo-jumbo. While I'm reluctant to try to explain a supernatural thing with a "natural" scientific method, I'm aware that we are all earthbound, and God is the god of science and nature as well as of the heavenly and supernatural.

Andrew Newberg, M.D., is an American neuroscientist who is the Director of Research at Myrna Brind Center for Integrative Medicine at Thomas Jefferson Hospital, an Adjunct Professor of Religious Studies, and an Associate Professor of Radiology at the University of Pennsylvania School of Medicine. He is also the author of *How God Changes Your Brain.*

In a study conducted in 2008, Dr. Newberg examined

people who speak in tongues by monitoring them with an MRI that reveals brain patterns. I encourage you to watch the results of his research with this link: (http://www.you-tube.com/watch?v=NZbQBajYnEc.)

Newberg, and others, have monitored the brain activity of subjects who are praying, both in earthly language and when they pray in tongues. Beyond scientific explanation, the brains of those speaking in tongues showed no brain activity on the monitors. Wait… let that sink in. They were alive, breathing, their hearts were beating. But when they spoke in tongues, monitors detected no brain activity.

Speaking in tongues, literally and scientifically, bypasses the human brain. This is what lets us have access to the Divine, getting our humble human mentality out of the way.

Let me offer a specific example. One of the members of my Bible study, Maya, was going through a challenging divorce. While she'd been a woman of means in her marriage, her husband left her with a little one. Because her ex—not unlike my own—was stingy and sly, Maya was concerned she'd not have the means she needed to care for herself and her son. But as he departed, he did leave her in possession of a very valuable car. Sadly, it was registered in his name only, so Maya was concerned that she'd be unable to retrieve its value. She wanted to transfer title to manage a cash flow problem. Because he was so miserly, she worried that her husband would be an obstacle to transferring the title. We held Maya up in prayer, both in our earthly language and by praying in tongues for her. When she went to the DMV to transfer the title, the lady asked her why she'd bothered to come to the DMV. Maya was naturally confused. She told the clerk that she was transferring this title because of a divorce. When the clerk replied, "The title in my terminal says this vehicle is already in your name," Maya was amazed. She'd looked at the paperwork. Her ex had not transferred the title. She knew what she had seen.

This was an answer to prayer that we would not have known even to ask for! We did not, in our earthly language, ask God to fix the title. It didn't even come into our imaginations. But by praying in tongues, we bypassed those limited imaginations and tapped into the great possibilities that God has to offer.

This is a miracle! No human changed the title. Nobody altered the terminal at the DMV. Only God can alter the natural world with supernatural phenomena. *When we pray, speaking in tongues, it releases miracles from heaven.*

## Activating others

When we become Christians, it's not a one-and-done proposition. We are not meant to accept God into our hearts and simply sit on what He gives us. Rather, we are meant to live to glorify God. It is my desire and intention that I will leave myself open to advancing God's kingdom every single day. This means, naturally, sharing the good news of Jesus Christ. It also means helping other believers to deepen their own relationships with God.

When I write these things about advancing God's kingdom, I worry that to some, I may sound like an oddball. But that is an earthly concern, not a spiritual one. I can live with being thought an oddball by others. All I am called to do is to share the Gospel, to testify that God is good. I cannot worry about what other people think of me. I'll leave that to God.

Being endowed with the Holy Spirit's gift of speaking in tongues has another empowering benefit beyond even the astounding connection to God. Once you access the supernatural aspects of faith, *nothing seems impossible*. By finding a route around the limitations of human understanding, we are all capable of embracing the abundance and intensity of what is possible through God.

The gifts of the Holy Spirit are available to all. So once each of us embraces them, we can activate others to have them too. Of course, others must welcome and invite this activation.

I recall a dear friend, Marina Tsang. Her husband,

Keith, was suffering from melanoma of the skull. To make matters worse, he had developed mysterious infections, leaving the doctors baffled about the treatment plan. Marina was deeply troubled by this, of course. I knew that what was needed was a deep and potent level of prayer. So I asked Marina's permission to activate her ability to speak in tongues. She welcomed this and gave permission. Remember, God gives us power, authority, and dominion; He cannot operate in our lives without our permission. And in just a moment after she gave the okay, she was rattling off prayer with sounds and syllables she'd never before uttered. With her husband's condition in mind, she prayed in this unknown tongue on his behalf. This was 6:45 p.m. on a Tuesday night. Within moments of her prayer, Marina received a call from her husband's nurse that the antibiotics were finally working and that the course of treatment could be developed. Praying in tongues is the most effective and efficient way to intercede for others by passing our minds from our spirits to the Holy Spirit.

Why is it so easy for me to activate others to speak in tongues? I have no special talent. I am no more powerful than any other person of faith. But the reason that I am able to do this is that I have no doubt. Faith with that degree of confidence is enormously powerful. Ever since I witnessed that circle of angels around me, my faith has grown. It is easy for me to say to another person, "You can speak in tongues too." It's easy because I've experienced being activated by those three people who laid hands on me that first day. It's easy because I have subsequently activated so many others to speak in tongues. They can testify the benefits of speaking in tongues too.

To learn to speak in tongues does not require you to study at a theological seminary. It does not require any tests or study, no software to download, no textbooks to buy. To speak in tongues, we need only to express what is already in our spirit. Then we merely need to move our tongues and vocal cords, allowing the sounds and language to flow through us without exerting logic, judgment or limiting it with doubt. We can each welcome this supernatural power.

We are each invited to experience this level of closeness with God and to gain the omniscience that He offers.

## Spiritual gift abandoned, spiritual gift reclaimed

Our walk with God is seldom a straight line, and that has been true for me as well. Though I was activated to speak in tongues in 1992, and even given that glorious vision complete with seven angels, I did not simply continue to speak in tongues with ease. For six months, I kept at it, and I experienced the joy and peace that comes with living in the presence of the Holy Spirit. But my mind fought with me.

Though my spirit had been blessed, my intellect argued. I just couldn't see the value of speaking in tongues. My mind just could not grasp it. So, for twenty years, I did not speak in tongues.

After years of not speaking in tongues, in 2012, I invited Peggy Cole, the prophetess, to host a prophetic meeting in that San Francisco condominium that God had prompted us to buy. She reactivated me, inviting the Holy Spirit to flow through me again. From then on, until this day, I have welcomed this mysterious and powerful gift. Better late than never, right?

As I began to practice it, welcome it, and surrender my intellectual arguments against it, the gift of tongues has brought enormous power to my life. I know, deep in my heart, deep in my spirit, that God wants every one of us (and that includes me, of course) to speak in tongues so that our spirits can communicate directly with God's spirit. When we do so, we are speaking in mysteries that I cannot understand with my finite mentality. I have to step out in faith to deal with matters of the unseen spiritual world. Speaking in the language of the angels lets us do that.

Since 2012 and my continued practice of speaking in tongues, I read the Bible with much more ease and understanding. When I read passages that once baffled me, I now have revelations about their meaning. My spirit is much more alert and sensitive. I can hear God's voice more easily. My spiritual eyes can see the unseen spiritual world much more clearly. My mind— once my enemy and a source of confusion—can now embrace and understand the mysteries of God. I see heaven open up to me, and I'm rid of my fears.

It is with the power of the Holy Spirit that we are best equipped for the spiritual warfare that we encounter. Satan has no power in the presence of the Holy Spirit. Temptations, worry, and fear find no harbor with us when we are filled with the Holy Spirit.

And perhaps one of the biggest blessings of all is that with the power of the Holy Spirit, we are empowered to activate others and to harvest souls to God's family as well as helping to strengthen fellow Christians.

*Then he answered and spoke to me saying, "This is the word of the Lord unto Zerubbabel saying, 'Not by might, nor by power, but in My Spirit, saith the Lord of Hosts.'" Zechariah 4:6 (KJV)*

I had shared testimony and prayed for a certain friend to find the Lord for thirty years, encouraging him to turn away from Buddhism and to become a Christian. Frankly, I'd given up on him. But not long after I began diligently practicing speaking of tongues, he contacted me and told me that he'd given up Buddhism and had accepted Jesus as his savior. I realized that through the power of the Holy Spirit and speaking in tongues that I'd employed heavenly allies in this earthly situation. He was called away to the Lord in mid-October 2020. I have peace because I know that he is now in the arms of our Heavenly Father. His soul was not lost.

Speaking in tongues has enabled me to have a closer walk with God. It enables me to live supernaturally in the natural world, and it both enables me and emboldens me to communicate easily with strangers on matters of God.

**Using the gift of tongues to testify for the Lord**

Just as we do not have to be in a house of worship to pray, we do not have to be at a revival meeting to bring souls to

God. Because I've been emboldened by the power of the Holy Spirit, I am no longer shy about testifying about God's glory and love, even to strangers.

I was once trying on clothing in a department store. The sales lady and I struck up a conversation about how difficult it was to be a single mother. She asked me how I seemed to have such joy and peace. When I told her that it was because I have Jesus as my savior, she said she wanted to have what I have. Right there in the changing room, she accepted Jesus into her heart.

While taking an Uber to go to an ophthalmology appointment at UCSF, the driver commented that I looked nice. It was a casual compliment, one to which a simple "Thank you" might be our only response. But the Lord prompted me to say more. The Lord said, *Tell her you used to buy clothes from the Salvation Army.* So I did. Then I complimented how lovely she looked in her outfit. She told me that she had bought hers at Goodwill because she was preparing for a job interview that afternoon. Emboldened by the Holy Spirit, I offered to pray for her about the job interview. Then I asked her to pray for herself. Somehow I had the sense that we did not really know precisely what to pray about. I suggested to her that we should pray in tongues because while we might not know exactly what to pray for, tongues is the perfect prayer because it bypasses our own understanding. My Uber driver then said, "I would love to speak in tongues, but I don't know how." So, when we'd reached my destination, and she'd stopped the car, I activated her, honoring her invitation. Just like that, she began speaking in beautiful, fluent tongues. Afterward, she told me that she felt great peace, joy, and assurance about getting that job.

Once in Hong Kong, a limo driver who picked me up from the airport told me that he remembered me from my visit the year before. He thought there was something special about me. The Lord prompted me to tell him that I was practicing speaking in tongues, and that is what gives me power, peace, and joy. The driver said he was a Christian, and he too wanted to speak in tongues and walk in the power of the Holy Spirit. So, I activated him. Easy as that.

I've been blessed to have the opportunity to activate my trainer at the Equinox Gym. She opened up in the most beautiful tunes like an angel singing. What an uplifting way to worship God. She sang angelic sounds, so beautiful, rhythmic, and angelic, the very first time she spoke in tongues. Some people are instantly fluent like that, and I had to fight my jealousy because when I first started speaking in tongues, it did not feel fluent; my spiritual channel was restricted by my skeptical mind. But as I've practiced tongues, I've learned to let go and increase the diameter of my mouth and throat to increase my outflow so that the Holy Spirit can pour out unrestricted.

There is no decision we can make that will have a greater impact on our lives than accepting God into our hearts and accepting Jesus Christ as our savior. This is our "golden ticket." This is how we establish a relationship with God and assure our eternal life in heaven. Once we accept Christ, we are co-heirs to the Kingdom of God. Jesus restores us to the position we held before the fall of man before Adam succumbed to the temptation of Satan.

It is through partaking of the gifts of the Holy Spirit that we transform our "natural" lives into the "supernatural" living that God has for us. We have available to us every spiritual gift, God's enormous, unfathomable love and power that is unimaginable.

Walking with God, endowed with the Holy Spirit, miraculous occurrences are commonplace. We can heal from past trauma. We can claim spiritual authority and have dominion over all that God has created for us. We can live in abundance and do so to the glory of God.

Look at the birds of the air; they do not sow or reap or store away in barns, and yet your heavenly Father feeds them. Are you not much more valuable than they? Who of you by worrying can add a single hour to his life? — MATTHEW 6:26-27 NIV

# Chapter 9

## How the Holy Spirit is Present in Our Financial Affairs

*You shall remember the Lord your God, for it is He who gives you the power to get wealth. Deuteronomy 8:18 (ESV)*

*I pray that you may prosper in all things and be in health, just as your soul prospers. III John 1:2 (NKJV)*

**Why is this last chapter? And why is it about money?**

**Stewardship, obedience, and the prosperity God has for us all**

For many years, when they noticed the financial blessings that God bestowed upon me, friends and family members urged me to write a book. What they wanted was to know my "secrets" for obtaining wealth. They wanted me to write a book and call it *How I Made My First Million with God as My General Partner.* But that title completely misses the main reason for talking about financial success, and it's the opposite of the reason I eventually decided to write this book. I've used plenty of examples of financial issues throughout this book, not because money is more important than other issues, but because it is what people look to me to speak about and one of the vehicles through which I have been trusted to testify about God's goodness. Throughout the process of writing this book, God has prompted these stories, so I trust that He would do so only because He wants this to be part of my testimony.

So why did I include matters of money in Part 3, the section about the Holy Spirit? I did this because it has been with the guidance, strength, and prompting of the Holy Spirit that I have attained wealth and grown it. So many people separate their career and business endeavors from their faith. I'm here to tell you that God, through the Holy Spirit, should be at the very center of our every endeavor, including, and especially, our financial pursuits. God's Spirit is mingled with our spirits in every endeavor of our lives.

It is always God's intention to prosper us; it's only a question of whether we want to listen to Him or not.

Yes, I have experienced success in real estate and making sound investments. But there would be no glorification of God by my writing about the buying and selling techniques I've employed or the kinds of investments I've profited from. That kind of how-to book is available in every bookstore. That's not the book God nudged me to write.

My prowess as a broker and as an investor does not come from any special skill or trade secrets. When God laid on my heart that I was to go into real estate, I knew nothing about it. He guided me to learn. I learned the mechanics of buying and selling real estate like anyone else might; I took community college classes; I studied, took tests, obtained legal certifications, gained experience, and learned from mentors to learn the practices. In other words, I honored God by working hard to do the best job I could do at the work He called me to do.

Had God prompted me to become a musician, a physician, an artist, or a mail carrier, He'd have provided me with the means and the skills to do those jobs well and, I'm convinced, to be just as successful—even financially so—just as He provided me the means to being a success in real estate.

*The real secret to my financial success has nothing to do with trade secrets; it has everything to do with seeking, listening to, and heeding God's voice. It has everything to*

***do with trusting God and obedience to Him.***

This is why this chapter on money follows only after the chapter about staying in constant connection with God through prayer and Bible study. Money without the presence of God in our lives can make us vulnerable to sin, vulnerable to relying on earthly values instead of Godly ones. But money—when acquired through God's guidance and managed with good stewardship—is a powerful thing and can be used for God's glory as well as personal security and comfort.

Learning to hear God's voice and staying connected with the infinite and wise lessons that the Bible has for us is not only the source of health, joy, and love in my life but also the source of welcoming God to prosper me. Yes, I talk about financial success, but not to brag about my wealth. After all, remember, the wealth itself is worthless unless used for God's glory. But I talk about wealth to testify about God's love and the prosperity that He has for us all.

Achieving wealth, even great wealth, is not the quality for which I want to be held in anyone's esteem. I want others to see me as a woman of God first and foremost. Money is a temporal thing of no value against the eternal riches that are available to us through God.

Because of my financial successes, others listen to me, and I believe—even more so now through the process of writing this book—that God wants me to make use of the financial blessings He has bestowed on me. If I were a great violinist, I would strive to use my instrument to glorify God through beautiful music. If I were a skilled painter, I could create art that shows God's glory.

Let me remind you here of John Harrison, the man with the million-dollar taste buds, whose job was ice cream tasting. God prospered him through that unusual (and delicious) career. God can prosper you, whatever your vocation, if you are seeking and heeding His divine guidance.

Whatever talent, skill, or accomplishment we achieve,

can be used to show God's love, mercy, and generosity. So, if by God's grace, I've developed skills for achieving financial abundance and security, which now provide me with a vehicle to share the Gospel and to testify to God's goodness, then that wealth has value, and I'm happy and grateful to serve God in this way. So I'm including this final chapter with a focus on money, not because money has any inherent value of its own, but because it allows me to testify to God's greatness in a way to which many can relate.

The focus here is not on the techniques of earthly business but the spiritual practice of surrender, submission, trust, and obedience. These are the techniques for approaching God. In Chapter 8, I talked at great length about being in God's presence through prayer, Bible study, and deepening our spiritual lives by accessing the gifts of the Holy Spirit. Here, in this final chapter, I'll talk about how that relates specifically to issues of money.

**Is it wrong to be rich?**

Many people wonder if it honors God to be wealthy, particularly when there exists so much poverty and suffering in the world. I'll admit that I believe that wealth—though of course preferable in many ways to leading a life of financial struggle—comes with it some new kinds of challenges when it comes to ourrelationship with God.

It's said that there are "no atheists in foxholes," by which it's meant that when we are in times of great need, it feels natural to seek God's help. Whether it is a marital crisis, a financial one, a health matter, or whatever difficulty we might be in, pain, worry, fear, and sorrow often bring us to our knees.

But it's been my observation that it is often more challenging to stay close to God, to seek His help during times of abundance. Those experiencing financial abundance and times of comfort are most at risk of losing track of God, of neglecting to seek His voice. Those who have wealth sometimes get egotistical, prideful, thinking that they have created the abundance that surrounds them. I believe this is what God meant in the following passage:

*It is easier for a camel to go through the eye of a needle than for a rich man to enter the Kingdom of God. Mark 10:25 (KJV)*

God would not discriminate, limiting admittances to heaven on the basis of income, of course. But with financial wealth, it becomes easier to lose track of our relationship with Him, to think that we no longer need guidance. God never steps away from us, but we can, and sadly do sometimes, step away from Him.

So to answer the question at the top of this section, *Is it wrong to be rich?* The answer is no. God wants us all to reap a generous harvest and to live in abundance. He just doesn't want us to be swallowed up by the rewards of the natural world and to lose track of His heavenly kingdom and our place in it.

**Money management is a spiritual discipline**

As I've mentioned previously, when God calls us to do a certain task, He always provides the resources for us to complete it. While determining the contents of this chapter about money, in my regular weekly Bible fellowship, we were simultaneously studying Rick Warren's "Financial Fitness" series. Now, some might call this a coincidence; I do not. I say that this is God at work, honoring my obedience in writing this book and providing me precisely the inspiration and information that I need to complete it.

Rick Warren is a pastor I've come to appreciate and admire. He speaks about complex things in simple, easy-to-understand ways. In his lessons called *"Financial Fitness,"*—Warren says: "Money management is a spiritual discipline that God is actually watching how I handle my wealth to see what He can trust me within the true spiritual riches in heaven."

Warren explains that in the Bible, more than half of the parables that Jesus offered as lessons were about money and financial stewardship. Jesus spoke much more frequently about money than he did about heaven or hell. Doesn't that seem curious? Warren goes on to explain why this is the case. "We spend more time thinking about money than we do heaven or hell," Warren says. Because money—making it, saving it, investing it, protecting it, giving it away—occupies so much of our time and energy, it dominates much of our lives. So, of course, Jesus offers us lessons about money.

It is simultaneously true that because so much of our daily lives revolve around financial issues, money is also the arena in which Satan can find ways to wheedle into our emotions and put a wedge between God and His children. Satan can spark greed, pride, financial fear, worry, material lust, or hoarding. All of these have nothing to do with the abundance and what God offers to every one of us.

As Pastor Warren tells us, all that we have on this earth is a loan, and this includes money. If we are very fortunate, we are allowed to "borrow" these things for a hundred-year lifetime. During our time on earth, we are to use our resources—all of them, including our time, our talents, and our money—to advance the Kingdom of Heaven. We are loaned these things, and at the end of life, we will be held accountable for how we've used money in our lives. Have we acquired it ethically, invested it wisely, given it generously, and used it to serve God and to help others? Have we sought and heeded God's guidance in all things, including our financial lives? Have we set aside our fears of scarcity and trusted God for His blessings and abundance?

Rick Warren says, "Money is the acid test of your faithfulness. God uses it more than any other thing in your life to test your faith." But Pastor Rick didn't make this concept up; he got it directly from the lessons Jesus taught us.

**Remembering the purpose of money**

I've heard it said that "The one who dies with the most toys wins." I suppose this saying is meant to be funny, but the humor is lost on me. This saying, however playfully intended, celebrates greed and the acquisition of material things. I ask you, how is God glorified in this? The answer is, of course, that God is not glorified by our amassing wealth simply for the sake of being rich. Nor is he glorified when we hoard money or material things.

We can talk to God about anything. We can ask God for anything. And yes, that also includes money. I prayed for the financial means to care for my children, and I prayed specifically for God to direct me to a way to acquire one hundred thousand dollars so that I could plan for their future educations and take care of their needs as I raised them. (Back then, $100K could do that.) But notice that my prayer was not, *God make me wealthy*. My prayer was, *God, please help me to provide well for my children.* I did not ask for crumbs; I asked for enough to provide for them well.

Money is simply a resource that God provides, just as He provides air, water, food, love, and time. Just as gluttony for food does not honor the abundance of the earth that God has given us, gluttony for money does not honor Him.

Even more crucial than these truths is to know that our earthly wealth, whatever amount it might be, and how we handle it is merely a demonstration of our faith and obedience, and the true reward is not an earthly one but an eternal one.

*Jesus said, "If you are untrustworthy about worldly wealth, who will trust you with the true riches of heaven? And if you are not faithful with other people's things, why should you be trusted with things of your own?" Luke 16/11 (NLT)*

### God gives in abundance

In Franklin Jentezen's sermon that we mentioned earlier, "God Wants to Prosper You," he gives us an important message:

***God is the God of abundance, but you'll never experience that until you believe God's abundance.***

God provides for His children with great abundance. The creation story in Genesis, which I've referenced several times, is a metaphor for His generosity. He didn't just give Adam and Eve a ratty little patch of a garden to live in. No, God created Eden. Eden was filled with every kind of flora and fauna, lush gardens, clear waters, and everything that the first humans could ever want. It was filled with great beauty, bursting with abundance, with the ability to meet their every need. And God also endowed man with dominion over it all, to be custodians of the entire natural world.

The creation story demonstrates that God *wants* to bless us. Like any loving father, He wants us safe, provided for, successful, comfortable, and joyful.

When God gave man dominion over the Earth, He also called upon us to be good stewards of the resources that He provides. Our bodies are a "resource" we are given; we are to take care of our body, regarding it as a temple. Nature's bounty is a resource; we should preserve, protect, and use natural resources without waste.

Money is simply another of the resources that God gives us, and like all others, we are to be good stewards over it. We are to seek His wisdom, guidance, and help in financial decisions.

In many societies today, those with wealth are elevated to a level of importance. Social status and conspicuous consumption are celebrated. Esteem granted to the wealthy, simply because of their wealth, is misplaced. In fact, to elevate another for this purpose is a kind of idolatry. When we *idolize* those with wealth or fame, or power, we do not honor God. I can feel people do that to me because of my financial success, and I shun it.

It bears repeating that the only real purpose of financial wealth is to glorify God and to advance God's kingdom on Earth. A person of wealth, someone on the A-list, featured in the society pages, is no more important to God than is a person of humble means. Whatever we are given, we are to manage it well and use it for God's glory.

## God as lender

Further in Pastor Rick Warren's talk that I cited earlier, he speaks of the financial means we are given in this life as a "loan" that God grants us. After all, it's often been said that you can't take it with you. We are loaned all that we have, and we are meant to honor our "lender" by using it wisely.

## Abundance vs. money lust

God always wants to bless His children. Just like earthly parents want their children to be happy, well provided for, and live comfortably, so too does our Heavenly Father.

But I invite you to imagine being a parent watching your children make poor choices with their money. They buy impulsively, don't care for the things that they buy, and then expect more money to come their way. While God wants us to have all that we need, He is not pleased with waste, with gluttony, with insatiability, or with greed or hoarding.

It is Satan that drives us to compulsions. Whatever God gives us, Satan says *More, more, more.* As soon as we see an item in a store (or now online), that flash of a feeling, *Buy it, buy it, buy it* arrives. That is not God's voice. Wastefulness, frivolous spending, and lust for temporal things are NOT God's abundance. That is gluttony and greed. Those do not come from God but from Satan.

Why do I talk about this here, directly following the chapter devoted to prayer? I do so because God is always available to us for guidance on all matters, big and small. He is there for us when those greed monsters whisper, *Buy it, buy it, buy it*. This is money lust. If we seek God's guidance in our purchases, we will make wiser choices, bypassing those things that are fool's gold, momentary distractions that we think will make us happy. He will instead guide us toward wise purchases, dissuade us from foolish ones, and help us to learn stewardship in all things, whether our bank account is modest or grand.

We've all heard of celebrities or lottery winners who have amassed huge amounts of money, only to later go bankrupt because of poor money management and a pattern of bad spending choices. And we've all known that family who has a modest income but manages it carefully, invests it wisely, and creates a secure future for themselves. Good stewardship is not about how much we have but how well we manage our resources. As we learn to manage small amounts and to glorify God with our thoughtful stewarding, we can be blessed with larger amounts.

What's most important to remember here is that it is through being in a constant conversation with God that we gain guidance on all decisions we face, including our decisions about spending, earning, and investing money. And of equal importance, God guides us about when and how to donate money or use it to help others.

**The three faces of stewardship: multiply, save, and give away without hoarding**

There are three parts to being good financial stewards: multiplying our resources (both earning and investing), saving them, and giving them away.

*Multiplying*

I've given you many examples of how God has given me chances to multiply my resources: by going into real estate as a career, by investing wisely in properties, and stocks, alternatives, and startups, and in making specific investments. Again, the purpose of multiplying our financial resources is to both take care of our needs—and our pleasure, too—and to advance God's ministry on earth.

*Please, do not forget the most important principle here: God always wants to prosper us.*

I like to think of earning money and spending or sharing it like inhaling and exhaling the air that we breathe. We inhale to provide the oxygen our bodies need; we earn money to provide for our monetary needs. We exhale that which our body does not need to hold onto; we spend money on our basic needs first, responsibly and intelligently.

How much sense does it make to hold your breath? None, clearly. When we have followed God's guidance that helps us to prosper, then as good stewards, we can spend on our needs and the pleasures that God provides for us to enjoy. When it comes to both how we earn and how we spend (and give), God is there for guidance and assistance.

If our walk with God is a close one, our prayer and study of the Bible frequent, and we strive to live righteously, we will have all the guidance we need about being good stewards.

I seek God's guidance for investments too. By this time in this book, I hope that when you read that last sentence, you say, *Of course, you do, Margaret! God is good. Why wouldn't you seek His guidance in all things?*

God wants us to invest wisely, to multiply our assets, and this lets us do more and more of His work on earth. Some of my contributions can be called "angel investments"— which can sometimes be very risky investments, of course—I rather like that heavenly reference in the world of money, don't you? When determining such investments, I must do my homework, research the ethics, the profitability, and the outcomes of each company in which I invest. Guided by prayer, prompted by the Holy Spirit, and having used the skills with which God has endowed me to research companies. I've been guided to be an angel investor in a real estate loan compliance software company, medical device companies, a firewall security company, a pharmaceutical company that creates medication for mental illness, Alzheimer's Disease, and many other such products.

What is amazing about these investments is that they are a win-win-win. The investment helps the companies create products and services that serve others; I am often rewarded with a substantial financial profit. Since it is God guiding me to do this, I am often brought opportunities to testify about God through the contacts I make.

It is important that we do not look at others through

the eyes of money. I do not regard anyone with wealth as any more important than one with more modest means. But the world does value wealth, and because I've been blessed (and you can be too), we can use the esteem of others as an opportunity to show others God's generosity and love. *Win, win, win.*

Does this mean that every one of my investments is a winner? Not at all. There are profits and losses, but I've come to trust that whether the investment pays off in financial dividends or not, the investments that God guides me to make are always profitable in serving Him.

Let me offer one small disclaimer. Please know that this is not a book of advice for making financial investments, particularly ones that could be risky, such as angel investments. These do not all prove financially profitable. My guidance here is that I invest when God guides me to do so through the Holy Spirit. I seek to support those organizations that serve others and help with problems. I choose to invest in companies that are well managed, that they too are good stewards of what they are given. But God's purpose is not always huge financial profits for each investment, as He has a higher purpose in guiding me to make each financial decision, and I have learned to trust in Him. Some of these investments lose money—a challenge to my faith—but I've learned that God's dividends are always generous when I act faithfully. Whether or not an individual investment has a big payoff or a loss, He ultimately cares for me and prospers me because of my faith in Him.

### Saving

Full stewardship of our money involves more than earning and spending. Saving and investing are also part of stewardship. If we spend everything we earn, we don't have the resources to handle the unexpected, take care of long-term needs, or save for special purchases or experiences. If we do not save, we also have no reserves for investing. Obviously, saving money is a part of responsible financial management and good stewardship. But do be cautious; there is a big difference between saving responsibly and hoarding out of greed, selfishness, or fear. Those qualities are not from God and are not good stewardship.

*The wise man saves for the future, but the foolish man spends whatever he gets. Proverbs 21:22 (LB)*

Stinginess and miserliness do not glorify God. To hoard money is like holding our breath and not expelling the bad air. The exhale is as important as the inhale. There is a balance to be found. We breathe in and supply ourselves with what we need; we breathe out and let go of what we do not need to hold onto. We work and earn money, invest well to multiply it, and then we spend on our necessities and our pleasures and use it in other ways to glorify God. It is good to be frugal and not wasteful, but it does not glorify God if we live in a state of deprivation when that comes as a result of hoarding, stinginess, or fear.

Earlier in this book, I told you that my first husband was a financially successful man. In fact, he was a workaholic. So multiplying his money was not a problem for my Ex; he generated a high income and invested it. But he was so obsessed with holding onto his money that he far surpassed frugalness; he hoarded his money. He deprived his family enough to meet even our basic needs. He wanted us to conserve utility bills, insisting that we did not need to use the heat (even in New Jersey winter), and told us to flush the toilet only once per day in a family of four. After we separated, and though he was well able, my Ex refused to pay his obligated spousal and child support, though it was a minimal amount.

To economize, to avoid waste, and to shun spending money excessively is good stewardship. We must avoid lust of the eye when it comes to our purchases. And I have also learned from my own mistakes in this way. Remember that ring I told you of earlier? I was lured, not by the idea of making a wise and prudent investment, but by the enticing idea that I was getting something rare and a "great deal" on it. I was lured by the temptation of getting an exceptional item. I have also to admit that I've needed to examine some of my own purchases in the past, and I've realized that sometimes I purchase something in order to impress others. After buying them, these purchases did not bring me joy but regret. When I spend thoughtfully and with God's guidance, even on a pleasure item, I feel at peace.

Fortunately, God is forgiving and has offered me many opportunities to learn and to relearn this lesson.

And they exceeded our expectations: They gave themselves first of all to the Lord, and then by the will of God also to us.
– 2 CORINTHIANS 8:5 NIV

## *Giving and philanthropy*

The third part of financial stewardship is giving money away. Giving money can be in the form of gifts, tithing to support the efforts of the Church, or philanthropy to support causes that we hold dear and that glorify God. Let's talk first about tithing.

I have told you how God intervened when I prayed for help in providing for my children after my divorce. But my first encounter with God concerning money actually took place years before that when I was in college, and it was not about obtaining money but making donations.

Our local church needed a bigger place to meet, so there was a big fundraising effort. As part of my church community, I prayed that God would provide for us. At the time, I did not have a great deal of money; I was one of those college students scraping to get by. I worked at a place called the Bear's Lair, the cafeteria in the student union at lunchtime at UC Berkeley, where I then attended. I also served as a waitress at night at the Davidson Hall dormitory just to make ends meet.

As I was praying about the circumstances for expansion in my church, God spoke clearly to me. He said, "Margaret, give the entire $400 you have in your savings account to your church." Today, that amount sounds so little, but it was a lot to me then. God reminded me, gently, at that time that I had once promised to give to Him all that I have in service of Him. And yes, He was right. I had made such a promise. So I obeyed God's nudging and contributed my entire savings to my church.

Many years later, after He called me to work in real estate, God blessed me with great abundance for my investors and indeed for myself as well. I was able (through God, not through my own powers) to obtain unprecedented returns. I always wonder why God chose me and my clients to prosper with such abundance. But now, God has answered this question for me.

*Remember the Lord your God. He is the one who gives you power to be successful... Deuteronomy 8:18a (NLT)*

That $400 was a test of my obedience and my stewardship over a small amount of money so that He could trust me with greater sums.

*Should people cheat God? Yet you have cheated me! But you ask, 'What do you mean? When did we ever cheat you?' "You have cheated me of the tithes and offerings due to me. You are under a curse, for you whole nation has been cheating me. Bring all the tithes into the storehouse so there will be enough food in my Temple. If you do," says the Lord of Heaven's Armies, "I will open the windows of heaven for you. I will pour out a blessing so great you won't have room enough to take it in! Try it! Put me to the test!" Malachi 3:8-10 (NLT)*

I'd forgotten all about that $400. But God never forgets.

In the writing of this book, God reminded me of that early incident of obedience. Because I honored God by donating to Him when I had little, He blessed me with much. So I continue to honor Him by giving to ministries and organizations that help to serve God.

God's voice has been with me throughout the writing of this book, prompting me to include items that I'd forgotten or not thought of for many years. God often reminds me of things I've forgotten. One day, He spoke to me, saying, *So much of our spending is to impress others... A lot of things you bought in the past were to impress others.* I really need to examine that. Have I bought clothing or décor or jewelry to impress others? How do I discern between God wanting to prosper me but not succumb to temptation, to pride, and to financial gluttony? Just because I *can* buy an item does not mean I *should* buy an item.

Remember, earlier in this book, I told you about my happy dress? This was the gown I bought to attend a fundraising event. Yes, that dress was an expense, but it was also of high enough quality and of a style that I could use and reuse many times at fundraising events that glorify God. In that dress, I can testify to God's abundance. But if I then use every event to fill my closet with more, more, more gowns, I am not glorifying God. I'm simply indulging in retail gluttony. So when the fashion writer commented that I'd worn that dress in the past, I could not be bothered with her pressure to purchase more. That is the temporal value, not the heavenly one.

The lust for more has a whole different feel than choosing to make purchases, with God's guidance and checking for prideful or greedy motives. Whether we are making purchases, modest or grand, for practicalities or for pleasures, we must always remember that we are using God's money, not our own. *When we are in God's will, seeking His guidance with our purchases, they give us joy without regret. When we buy out of lust or to please others, we feel no peace.*

In earlier chapters, I talked about various career and financial decisions that I've made—some of them wise and to the glory of God, others driven by my own agenda. When I ignored God's voice, listening to my own agenda as I did when I guided my clients to invest in those Texas Towers, I did not honor God. I put my clients at risk of a disastrous result. Had I obeyed God's nudging about that deal, my clients would have praised me. Because I did obey God's guidance when it came to the Marysville property, I was able to bring someone else to the Lord. I bought a ring out of lustful desire, and it has given me not a moment of peace. But the beautiful gown I bought, the one I've worn many times at events that glorify God, I've had nothing but pleasure.

Whatever we do, however, we spend money, it should be an opportunity to advance God's kingdom, even if we do not understand how that is the case. If we are listening to God's voice in our purchases and investments, He will guide us to the end that He hopes for us.

I sometimes look at my beautiful life, my loving

husband, the comfort in which we live, and I wonder why God has chosen to prosper me so. The truth is that God is good. It's as simple as that.

I am not unique. I have no particularly unique skills or intelligence, feeling myself average in so many ways. But what I have is an unlimited supply of guidance from one who is omniscient, omnipresent, and omnipotent. You can search for earthly mentors, and indeed their knowledge of the world may prove helpful. But the ultimate mentorship and the best possible guidance you can get is that of seeking God's guidance in all of the choices in your life.

*For God does not show favoritism. Romans 2:11 (NLT)*

### Tested by fire

As I mentioned earlier, I'm completing the writing of this book during not only the coronavirus pandemic but at a time when California, where I live, is enduring a rash of treacherous wildfires. Having lived for many years in San Francisco, I've always had the concern about earthquakes, so I still harbored concerns about my home in San Francisco. But now, wildfires have become even more of a threat, and that threatens the home in Sonoma.

On September 28, 2020, Ted and I were in our Sonoma home. At about 8:30 in the evening, our neighbors started calling us, saying that we may have to evacuate. So Ted and I put a few things together and left them at the front door. We know that fire can strike quickly. The Holy Spirit prompted me to take our two cars out of the garage and line them up facing out of the driveway so that at a moment's notice, we could drive straight out. At 10:30 at night, I got a call saying that our area should be prepared to evacuate.

I was scheduled to lead Bible study the next morning, so rather than wait, Ted and I decided to go to our San Francisco home (remember, the one God prompted us to buy) then, rather than wait for orders.

It's funny how the practicalities and logistics come to

us in these times, and because the fire was a high possibility, Ted wanted us to take both cars just to be on the safe side. I've mentioned I'm an early riser, but that also means that I tend to go to bed early and am not at my best after about 9 p.m. I prefer not to drive at night due to slight vision impairment. And Ted wanted me to drive the larger car, one that I've only driven a few times. With all of those factors at play, I found that I was tense, and worried, intimidated, and thinking that I could not do it.

But I drove. God's lessons to me over the years have been many, and despite my nervousness, I've learned that fear does not come from God. I was driving against all of my fears of being inadequate for the task. Before I left, I prayed about the wildfire in my own natural language. I prayed for our neighbors, for their safety, and for the safety of their property. I prayed for the firefighters. I called a neighbor who lives alone to confirm that she was okay. The road was congested with evacuees. Gas station lines were long. Anxiety started to overtake me. So, because my fear was great and I was no longer sure what to pray for, I began to speak in tongues. Immediately, a peace—the kind that God promises that "passes all understanding"—washed over me. For the entire ninety minutes of the drive, not only did I have peace but I was also given another blessing. Usually, speaking in tongues sounds like a foreign language—like gibberish to our human ears. But this time, I was also granted the interpretation of the prayers.

The interpretation was this: God reassured me that both of the houses we'd bought at His divine urging would come to no harm. He said that they would not suffer any damage because whatever God initiates, God will protect.

The comfort I felt for the remainder of that drive was such a blessing. And while I drove, with Ted driving in front of me, I saw the guardian angels that had come to protect us.

Why do I share this story in the chapter devoted to money? It's because we need to know that when God directs us and we are obedient to Him, He also protects us. This is not to say that only the homes of ungodly, disobedient people get burned in fires, of course. And in fact, it can be a test of our faith when we see bad things happen to the most faithful among us. Even in the stories of the Bible, we see that the most faithful are tested: Job, Noah, Daniel, and of course, Jesus Himself. But what is also true is that though these and other biblical figures, as well as modern-day Christians, endured trials and hardships, God was, and is always with them, honoring their sacrifices, their obedience, and their faith.

Knowing this does not mean I will never suffer losses or endure difficulties. But it is ours to keep the faith that God is always with us whatever circumstances prevail, His protections surround us, and the outcomes are in His hands.

Cast all your anxiety on him because he cares for you.
– 1 PETER 5:7 NIV

**The best insurance policy**

The next day after we'd evacuated from the fires, I called a dear friend whose house sits right in the middle of the wildfire's path. She told me that she feels secure because she has a special insurance plan called CHUBB insurance and that the CHUBB organization sent out three water trucks to spread fire retardant on her home. Neighbors near her lost their homes, and she did not.

After that phone call, I started to wish that we had CHUBB insurance too. I had tried to obtain a policy in 2018 after an earlier round of devastating fires but was then told that they were no longer writing policies for our area. But then, I recalled the Lord's reassurance as I'd fled the night before. I sat still and listened. And God said to me, *I am your insurance. I'm better than CHUBB. Stop worrying.*

I know it's the title of this book, but I can't stop saying it—God is good!

**To whom much is given—using our money to serve God**

Throughout this book, I've talked about seeking God's guidance on family matters—marriage, divorce, raising my children—and regarding the financial matters of earning, saving, investing, and spending money. I've confessed to the times when I disregarded His guidance, thinking that I knew better or ignoring His guidance when I had a different agenda. The results are painfully predictable.

As a result of learning to heed God's guidance on financial matters, I've been blessed with financial security and financial abundance. ***But it is crucial to note here that the only purpose of wealth is that we can use it to further the mission of God's Kingdom here on Earth.*** While God, like any loving parent, wants us to enjoy security and abundance, He also does not want our drive for wealth to eclipse what is truly important.

Just imagine that you are a parent. You have supported and guided your children in their education and in developing a career. Perhaps you even gave or loaned money for your children to start a business and, as a result, they have achieved great wealth. Then you discover that they used the money frivolously. They waste money on excessive spending and on endeavors that you know are not in their best interest. And you also notice that while your children have achieved great wealth, they are driven by greed for more, they are willing to compromise their ethics for profitable deals and have garnered a reputation for being stingy with clients, loved ones, and the community. As a parent, you can imagine how heartbreaking it would be to see your adult children with this relationship to their money.

I imagine that this is how God feels when He sees one of His children exercising poor financial choices. Money, like our bodies, like the treasures of nature, and like our talents and intellect are all resources of which God desires us to be good stewards. Mistreating or misusing these resources does not glorify our Heavenly Father; it does not advance the Kingdom of Heaven.

I've often heard one scripture misquoted regarding money. I hear that "Money is the root of all evil." This would imply that God wants us to be poor, wants us to struggle. I ask you, what loving father would desire for his children to suffer? Scripture tells us over and over that this is not at all God's desire. Today, many portray God as a vengeful, angry, cruel God that desires to punish us all. This is not at all the case.

So let's look more closely at the scripture that has been so often misquoted:

*For the love of money is the root of all kinds of evil. And some people, craving money, have wandered from the true faith and pierced themselves with many sorrows. I Timothy 6:10 (NLT)*

It is not money itself that is evil's root; it is the *love of money* and wandering from the true faith that results in the deepest stabs of sorrow for us. So while we pursue careers and make investments to ensure our financial security, and while we remain in constant contact with God about being good stewards of what He provides, we must always keep in our sights that money itself has absolutely zero value in God's Kingdom. It is valuable only for the purpose of serving Him.

If we are to serve God with our words, with our actions, with the lives that we lead, wouldn't it be logical that we would serve Him with our money as well? God helped me with the "supply" of my wealth; it is therefore incumbent upon me to glorify Him in both how I spend and invest and how I use the money He's provided to advance His holy Kingdom and to be a beacon for God's glory. My wealth is not "self-made"; it has been achieved only through God's guidance and goodness.

One of the ways that we can advance God's Kingdom is with financial support. Please note that donating money through tithe is *only one* of our ways to serve God. Prayer, giving testimony, sharing God's Word, spreading the gospel: these are as valuable as gold. But in our lives here on Earth, some of God's work is benefited by financial contributions. Our financial contributions to advance God's Kingdom come in three forms: tithing, philanthropy, and personal charity.

It's important to add here that God provides guidance, not only for how we should obtain and invest money but also for how we should tithe and donate our money. Just as with every decision I make in life, I strive to seek God's input regarding how I should use the wealth He's provided to me for His glory. I want to give to charities that are also good stewards of money so that the contribution has maximum benefit to those it serves. So I look for organizations where the bulk of the money goes to those in need, not to administrative costs. Charitable giving in God's eyes is not just zipping off a check; it involves thoughtful consideration and should always be done with prayer and God's guidance.

A friend of mine is always touched by the plight of the homeless that are so prevalent on the streets of far too many cities in America. For whatever reason that these people became homeless—some through unfortunate events, others through mental illness or drug addiction—she feels compassion and wants to help them when she sees them on the street or at traffic lights.

But my friend is also aware that some of these needy people are not capable of managing money, that if you give it to them, it could put them at risk for being harmed by others also desperate for money, and that some would use the money she'd give them only to purchase drugs or alcohol. Rather than give them money directly, my friend has chosen another way. She collects small bottles of toiletries (sometimes from hotels she stays in on business travel or when she sees good bargains), socks, long-lasting food items like nutrition bars, and other comfort items. She puts these into sealed bags that she keeps in her car and gives them to those she encounters in parking lots or on street corners. This way, the recipient is helped, but in a way that truly helps them and does not put them at risk of harm. Of course, donating to organizations that prevent homelessness or treat addiction or mental illness is another way to help this worthy cause. Assembling and distributing these small parcels is a way, within my friend's means, that she can offer immediate help. This is an example of responsible stewardship and of giving in a way that truly helps.

## Tithing

*For the love of money is the root of all kinds of evil. And some people, craving money, have wandered from the true faith and pierced themselves with many sorrows. 1 Timothy 6:10 (NLT)*

The Bible makes many references to tithing—contributing a portion of our earnings to support the ministry of the Gospel. In the above verse, it said we are to tithe to the storehouse of God's temple. Tithing is different from charitable contributions or philanthropy. Sometimes we wonder whether it makes a difference to God or not if we tithe. Here, God says we are to "Try it and put Him to test." He is serious about our tithing. I always seek God's input as I select the ministries to support. God has guided me to donate to various ministries that further His message, many of which I have cited in this book.

For some, tithing takes the form of regularly donating a portion of their income to their local church community. I tend to contribute to both local church and global ministries. The important thing is to seek God's guidance and to contribute to those ministries that truly serve God. Are they good stewards? Do they use the money to further the mission of spreading the Good News of God?

It's crucial here to know that God does not seek big showy acts of generosity that glorify the giver. God values the authenticity of the spirit with which we give, no matter the amount. The parable of the "widow's mite" is a touching story of Jesus teaching us the true meaning of giving.

*And Jesus sat over against the treasury, and beheld how the people cast money into the treasury: and many that were rich cast in much. And there came a certain poor widow, and she threw in two mites, which make a farthing. And he called unto him his disciples, and saith unto them, Verily I say unto you, that this poor widow hath cast more in, than all they which have cast into the treasury:*

*For all they did cast in of their abundance; but she of her want did cast in all that she had, even all her living. Mark 12:41-44 (KJV)*

In these verses, wealthy people made sizable contributions to the coffers of their synagogue—and they did so conspicuously, which makes their motives suspect. But this widow, who had little, donated two "mites." A mite was the smallest in value of all currency of that day. Two of them would be little more than a penny today. But Christ lauds this widow, stating that her contribution was of greater value because she had so little to give and that she

225

wanted to honor God with all that she had.

Remember when God prompted me to tithe $400 when I was a struggling student? That amount would be very little for me today, but then it was a great deal. It was a high percentage of what I had. In fact, it was all that I had in my savings at the time. By obeying God's prompting, I now more deeply understand that I was honoring Him. I was demonstrating my trust that He would provide for me.

He most certainly has kept that promise.

### *What is charity?*

In addition to tithing, we are also called to be loving and charitable.

*And now abideth faith, hope, charity, these three; but the greatest of these is charity. I Corinthians 13:13 (KJV)*

In other versions of the Bible, the word "charity" in this verse is translated as "love." While scholars can argue about that word's perfect translation from the original text, I choose to say that it does not matter. Charity is an expression of love. Love is charitable and kind.

We are all called to be charitable, regardless of our income, and in some cases, one's charity isn't about money at all. One can donate time, talent, compassion, and care all without spending money at all.

Because God has blessed and prospered me so generously, I have long felt it incumbent upon me to serve Him, to demonstrate His love through financial, charitable giving. I have learned that even in this, I must seek God's guidance. My selection of when, how much, and to whom I make charitable contributions must not be driven by my own desires or even by my emotions. Giving, even to causes that seem important, without God's guidance can lead to poor selections. As we should be good stewards of the money that we spend, we must also be good stewards of the money that we donate.

God is always available for consultation through prayer, and this is my guidance for charitable giving. That said, I do believe that experiences in our lives prompt us to be aware of certain needs. Let me offer a few examples.

### God's guidance for philanthropy

Sometimes God prompts me to donate money to various causes that cross my path. We don't want to waste money by giving it to poorly run organizations or to those who will not value it. We want to make sure that we are supporting causes and organizations that honor God. Some promptings come out of the blue; others are inspired because of a personal experience or a single encounter.

When my son, Samuel, suffered a head injury and Traumatic Brain Injury in 1978, I became intimately aware of the challenges that such patients and their families face. God saw fit to heal Samuel and, against all of the odds offered by the medical professionals (skilled though they were), Samuel not only recovered but also has achieved a level of independence that none of his doctors believed would happen, even living in Shanghai on his own, and becoming quite successful. (You and I know how that happened, of course.)

God laid it upon my heart that I should contribute generously to Traumatic Brain Injury (TBI) treatment and to endow Geoffrey Manley, MD, a world-renowned brain surgeon at San Francisco General Hospital and University California San Francisco. I did not hesitate. This endowed chair let us create twenty centers throughout the United States so that people in their location could more instantly receive treatment and early detection of TBI; when it comes to TBI, every second matters.

As a result of creating these centers, many people, including children like my Samuel, in locations around the country have benefited, including some high-profile people. Congresswoman Gabby Giffords suffered a severe brain injury when she was shot in the head at an event that took the lives of six other people, including a nine-year-old girl.

Her injuries were substantial, and she continues to this day to have an impairment. But because there was a center near her, her life was saved, and the subsequent rehabilitation has allowed her to reclaim her voice, her ability to walk, and a quality of life with her family. Now, the same quality of care that is available in San Francisco is available in multiple locations throughout the country.

If you feel moved to add to the efforts to treat TBI, you can contribute by going to makeagift.ucsf.edu/TBI. On this site, you can also find Impact Reports so that you too can be a good steward, assessing the value of your contribution.

## Finding purpose in pain

When we are going through a time of anguish, it is often difficult to understand how any good can come of it. But God is so magnificent that He can make use of any difficulty and can turn our anguish into good. Many times, God makes use of our personal experiences to prompt our charitable giving because our experience gives us empathy and understanding for others going through similar circumstances.

This is why I was so happy when God led me to endow a chair of traumatic brain injury to the world-renowned Neurosurgeon Dr. Geoffrey T. Manley, MD, Ph.D. Though the money came from my own bank account, I am aware that the funds I donated were not my own but simply on loan from God, handed to me to do His work and help others.

Following my contribution, I received a letter, which contained an "Impact Report," it itemized the many ways that this endowment was working to help others. I had all of the validation I needed that God had directed me to make this donation and that He was working more miracles for more families as a result.

My donation, leveraged along with other philanthropic partners, has helped scientists to increase knowledge about TBI and to educate patients and families in ways that I was not when Samuel was injured. The endowed chair has resulted in Level 1 Trauma Centers opening nationwide. Now blood tests that can identify biomarkers so that TBI can be more immediately diagnosed—crucial when dealing with brain injury—are available to many more people across the country. From research to treatment to education, God has used this money to ease suffering, and it all sprang from the experience I had when my son was small. God can use anything for good.

What I now know is that those who suffer TBI from accidents, gunshots, sports injuries, and even domestic violence are vulnerable to a whole host of other problems: induced mental illness, addiction, and personality changes. We want to prevent this as much as possible, and rapid, skilled treatment is the key. Along with that, knowledge about TBI is crucial. For people who have had immediate treatment and follow-up, the recovery rate is higher, and recovery is more holistic. I want the knowledge to be out there.

God makes use of my other experiences—my Chinese culture, my family, my children, and in my community—and through the Holy Spirit, I'm prompted to charitable giving. My experience in my first marriage made me sensitive to the needs of mothers entering or re-entering the workplace, either after leaving abusive marriages or overcoming other hardships. So I've been blessed with opportunities to contribute to programs that help them.

The coronavirus pandemic has robbed so many performing arts organizations of their funds, and the Holy Spirit put it upon my heart that the San Francisco Symphony is among them.

Though the experiences of an abusive marriage, a tragically injured son, and the culture in which I was raised gave me empathy. This is part of the "spirit," the emotional part of me. And while God uses this empathy to make me aware of the needs of others, it is not only from my emotions that charitable decisions are made. Without seeking God's will in prayer, our emotions alone can misguide us, can lead us to make impulsive choices, or can have us donating to causes that seem worthy but that are poorly managed or have other purposes. Without God, our emotions are a place that Satan can "play" his tricks and can seduce us into giving for our own glory. But when we surrender our will to God and seek His guidance, He can make use of our empathy, our "charity," our "love," and guide us to help others in circumstances that we may once have suffered.

## Giving doesn't end with the money

Being good stewards of our charitable giving doesn't end with writing the check. For some, this means that they participate in fundraising to multiply our gifts to a given organization. Sometimes, it means participating in special events, celebrations, or cleanup/building efforts. Because I have skills with money, I often volunteer to siton the boards of organizations to which I donate so that I can research and support their good financial practice. Giving money also requires good diligence.

## God really is THAT good

As I've grown and matured as a Christian, I've learned one crucial thing: *We must involve God in every single aspect of our lives.* Too many think of their relationship with God only on Sunday mornings or when they're faced with hardship or crisis. They may even pray a blessing at mealtimes or before retiring at night.

God is there to guide us in our intimate matters of love, family, and friendship. He is there in times of heartbreak and pain. God is with us when we are low and equally with us during times of celebration. And God must be part of our financial lives as well. Without His divine guidance, any prosperity we achieve is meaningless and an opportunity for temptation. He wants to prosper each and every one of us; I am no exception, just an example of His immeasurable goodness.

# My Cherished Desire

*The Lord is good, a strong refuge when trouble comes. He is close to those who trust in him. Nahum 1:7 (NLT).*

Throughout the pages of this book, I've shared my personal testimony—the guidance and direction that God has taught me in my walk with Him. Some of what I've shared has been big, practical guidance to a path of success, and other ideas have been small. No matter, God is there for every facet of our lives. I simply cannot imagine my life without God at the center of it—as my guide, as my companion, as my purpose. It is my joy to share the story of the goodness of God in my life.

God is not a Special Occasion or a Sunday-only God; He is an every day, every minute God. His love and guidance are available to us all. He wants us to live healthy, happy lives free of worry and enjoying great joy and abundance. That is the message of this book—God is good. It is my deepest hope that God is glorified by my sharing it.

God told me that He wanted me to write this book. I have many excuses. Not only do I not like to write, but I also do not write well, and English is my second language. Among all my excuses, I heard his message clearly. So, even though I struggled and hesitated, I began the process.

In late 2019, I even set the project aside for a bit, having talked myself out of the book project. Then in early 2020, the coronavirus swept the globe and sent us into our homes. It was then that I could no longer ignore God's urging. During the fears and worries that arose during the pandemic, God's voice was so very clear. He reminded me to choose God's favor over fear. He reminded me that if He called me to do something that He would also provide the way for me to do it and that through the Holy Spirit, God would guide me. He reminded me that He has helped me to do hard things many times. He helped me when He called me to sell real estate when I knew nothing about the field. He called me to have faith in Him when my son was in an accident and was in a coma. He called to me when I was in an abusive marriage and when I was afraid that I could not be freed of it. And He called me to trust him when I met (and at first disregarded) the man who would subsequently become the most loving husband I could have imagined. So why would He not provide me with the resources I needed to write and publish this book? The answer is obvious—of course, He would. And He has.

During this era of COVID, God reminded me of what a gift every day is and that we must make every one of them count. Perhaps the coronavirus serves to remind us of the preciousness of our lives and days on this earth. We create a meaningful, purposeful life by seeking to serve and glorify God every day and by listening to and following His guidance.

This book is designed solely for the purpose of glorifying God and testifying to others about his infinite love and His goodness.

**My sincere wish**

It is my sincerest wish that this book will bring comfort and encouragement to anyone struggling in their walk with God. Perhaps it will inspire some readers to welcome the supernatural powers of God into their lives. Perhaps it will give them peace. Maybe it will guide them to stop tolerating abuse or to feel the confidence to enter a new career field with God's gentle, loving guidance right alongside. And maybe, it will guide someone filled with doubts to find their faith, accept Jesus into their hearts, and embrace God as their own.

Truly, nothing could make me happier.

I am the LORD your God, who brought you up out of Egypt.
Open wide your mouth and I will fill it. — PSALM 81:10 NIV

## Bonus blessings for obedience

Many beautiful things have resulted from my obedience to God in writing this book. Because I needed to write both my experiences and my understanding of God's presence in my life, I needed to seek God's infinite wisdom and clarity about the topics I was to discuss in these pages. I've sought to keep open the channel of communication with my Heavenly Father so that I'm doing His will for His glory in writing. As a result, my prayer life has deepened, and my relationship with God has also deepened.

Through this deeper communion with God, I've experienced even more of His grace and new levels of freedom from worry and from resentments about the past. God's voice grows clearer and clearer to me, not because I'm anyone special; God speaks to us all if only we learn to seek His voice and listen to His reply. But His voice grows clearer because I am doing what I need to do to keep the channel open from my side. I'm seeking His voice in a constant way.

It really is as simple as that; we must keep ourselves open to hearing God's voice.

Through the writing of this book, I've been able to reflect upon my past that includes times when I heeded God's prompting and when I ignored it. I've been able to see when my motivations were pure and when my ego drove my decisions. I've been able to remember past suffering but have been gloriously freed of its hold upon me.

This book has proved a blessing in strange packaging to me. But the benefits to me are only the gravy; the meat of why I wrote this book is God and His message to all of us.

My goal in writing this book is neither financial nor recognition. My one and only goal in writing and publishing this book is to offer testimony that God is good and that His love is immutable and available to all, that His power is available to us through the Holy Spirit, and that we are forgiven through the blood of Jesus. God prompted me to tell this as a story that exemplifies His grace, his mercy, and the abundance He wants for all of His children. My exceptional life is really no exception; it is available to all.

*Oh, taste and see that the Lord is good; Blessed is the man who trusts in him. Psalm 34:8 (KJV)*

Should you wish to accept Jesus as your Savior now, it is very easy. You just have to believe in your heart that Jesus died for your sins and confess with your mouth that God has raised Him from the dead; you shall be saved.

*Whosoever calls on the name of the Lord shall be saved. Romans 10:13 (KJV)*

*That "whosoever" means you.*

If only one person reads this book and finds his or her way to God, then every hour spent writing it is worth the effort. If that person happens to be you, then you are the answer to my prayers.

# From the Mouth of Babes—
## Samuel Liu, My Son

When sorting through some of my files, just before publishing this book, I found a letter, written by my son when he was just 14 years old. The letter at the time was heartbreaking, and indeed it still moves me to read it, even after so many years. I believe that God guided me to find this small piece of paper at this moment to both offer validation for wanting to end my marriage back then, and indeed, as confirmation of the value of writing this book and sharing so much of my personal story in it. I am choosing to share these words from my son with you.

As I've said throughout this story, when God guides us to do something, He also provides the means for us to do it and the comforts we need along the way.

*The following is printed just as Sam wrote it.

*"Through the years, there have been many people who have influenced my life.*

*One of the most extraordinary people I have ever met is a woman. She had married a tight-budgeted man. Even though she had come from a well-off family in Hong Kong, she never asked her father for money. She took care of 2 children, a girl and a boy. She love them both dearly so much. It would tear her heart to scold them. In the East coast, she took the responsibility of being a mother, a school teacher, a wife, a housekeeper, and a Christian. As a wife, she was unhappy, because the man she had married often beat her or have rough vocal arguments. In 1975, the family moved to the West. She rebuilt her house. Since the children were older now, she taught them how to clean a* *house. It took a couple of years before she was free to look for another job. Since teaching jobs were so hard to come by, she took a hobby in real estate. After a half a year of training, she got her licence. She began selling houses. The next year, a tragedy overtook the house. The wife and her husband split up. She was strong in her soul, as they battled back and forth in court. She won, 1/2 of the battle, the kids. Soon the alimony and the child support checks stopped coming. With almost no money, she began selling land, shopping centers, and others. Her part time hobby became her 24-hour job. The next year, her son was hit by an automobile. She still worked hard, but now she had an extra loan on her back. She vigorously prayed as her near-death son lay there in comatose. After 5 weeks, the doctors thought she was crazy, she never gave up hope and always visited and prayed for him each day. Finally, after 6 weeks, he woke up. She finally rested for an <u>instant</u>. She had many wealthy Hong Kong buyers, who bought land in Texas. So she constantly travels to Dallas. To make a long story short, she became quite wealthy and married a very wise man. She sent her daughter to Phillip Exeter Academy. The amazing woman name is Margaret Liu Collins, my mother. Now she just want the best for both of her kids."*

# Resources and Inspirations

I have been the beneficiary of the work of many inspired and scholarly teachers and devote a great deal of time reading, listening to, and watching them share their understanding of God's Holy Word and our Christian Walk. I've cited many of these throughout the text of this book, always wanting to give credit where it is due. But I must also say that I'm sure that my own understanding has been informed by so many and over so many years that it is difficult for me to discern which of the teachers, writers, preachers, and others deserves credit. Here is a list of many resources that have informed my walk with God. Where I've quoted their ideas specifically, I've noted it. But in general, these teachers have provided me with great inspiration, great comfort, and insights. Below is a partial list of those whom I've credited specifically in this book or who have generally influenced my understanding. I owe these teachers much gratitude.

**Kynan Bridges**

*90 Days of Power Prayer: Supernatural Declarations to Transform Your Life*

**Randy Clark:**

*The Power to Heal*

*Ministry Team Training Manual*

*The Essential Guide to the Power of the Holy Spirit*

*There is More*

**Randy Clark and Bill Johnson**:

*The Essential Guide to Healing*

**Mike Connell:**

*Spiritual Authority*

*Gifts of the Holy Spirit*

*Deliverance and Healing*

*Hearing the Voice of God*

*Speaking in tongues*

*Wage a Good Warfare*

*How God does Miracles*

*Authority in the Family*

*Relationship or Rights*

**Kenneth E. Hagin:**

*Speaking in tongues*

*How You Can be Led by the Spirit of God*

*The Name of Jesus*

*Believer's Authority*

**Robert Henderson**

*Operating in the Courts of Heaven*

**Benny Hinn**

*Good Morning, Holy Spirit*

**Bill Johnson:**

*Hosting the Presence*

*The Mind of God*

*Developing Supernatural Lifestyle*

*When Heaven Invades Earth*

*The Supernatural Power of a Transformed Mind*

*Experience the Impossible*

**Guilleromo Maldonaldo:**

*Divine Encounter of the Holy Spirit*

*The Glory of God*

*The Kingdom of Power – How to Demonstrate Here and Now*

*How to walk in the Supernatural Power of God*

**Myles Munroe:**

*Kingdom Principles*

*Rediscovering the Kingdom*

"Understanding the Purpose and Power of Prayer" https://youtu.be/1DpmlL4cR_Y

**Joel Osteen**

*I Declare 31 Promises to Speak over Your Life*

**Derek Prince**

*They Shall Expel Demons*

*Blessings or Curse You Can Choose*

*Pulling Down Strongholds*

*Spiritual Warfare*

**Charles Stanley:**

*Life Principles of Bible*

**Art Thomas:**

*Paid in Full*

*Healing Miracles for Your Family*

**Cindy Trimm**

*Commanding your Morning*

**Andrew Wommack:**

*The Believer's Authority: What you did not learn in the church*

*Spirit, Soul, and Body*

*You have already got it*

*God Wants You Well*

*A better Way to Pray*

# Acknowledgments

I'm grateful to God for the everyday empowerment, encouragement, advocating, and love that He provided through the Holy Spirit, not only in my daily life but specifically in the writing of this book. Without the encouragement and prompting of the Holy Spirit, I would not have been able to complete this book

My husband Ted Collins provides me with enormous love and the most positive support any wife can hope for. He has also proved to be a loving, understanding, and patient stepfather to my children. I'm grateful for his loving and kind companionship. With his wonderful, steadfast presence, I'm able to live a productive and fulfilling life in ways I could never have imagined. I cannot imagine my life without him.

Betsy Graziani Fasbinder, a most respected ghostwriter, worked patiently and tirelessly to listen to and understand my story. She translated my thoughts into these written words. She helped me to write this book, expressing myself and my relationship with God in ways I would have been utterly unable to on my own.

Special thanks to Mike Waters, the creative artist of Joyful Toons (www.joyfultoons.com), who provided the charming cartoon images in this book. It's fun to add a bit of whimsy to this story. God does have a sense of humor, after all, and Mike helped to show it.

In the final revisions of this book, I could have asked no more of Pastor Terry Haggins than he offered. He gave a great deal of time and brought both scholarly insight and a scrupulous eye to help me to bring the work to a lovely polish. I hold enormous gratitude for his help. Susan Daijo offered a keen eye, immense patience, and tireless effort in confirming the precise quotations and citations for the many biblical selections used in this book. It's important to be precise and accurate in such things, and Susan, with her scrupulous eye for detail, helped me to do that.

To Phoebe Pao, many thanks for her artful and insightful translation skills and sensitivity to this material. I'm thrilled to be able to share this story with Chinese readers.

I owe great gratitude to my own parents, who've now both passed away, who gave me life and guidance and made great sacrifices for me. They were role models, mentors, and teachers in my secular life.

My daughter Magdalene, her husband Andrew, and my son Sam are God's gifts to me. Seeking God's best for them compelled me to seek a deeper, more intimate relationship with God and greater faith in His protective and healing power. I will forever hold them in my prayers. My love is unceasing, and they are always in my heart.

I'm immensely grateful for my stepdaughters, Blair and Lisa, their husbands Todd and Dave, and my grandchildren Chauncey, Peter, Case, Calum, and Reeve. Their love, respect, honor, and support are the sunlight and joy of my life.

Thanks to John and Winnie Vong, and to Debby Chen, who were the initiators of this book.

Thanks to Allison Storey, graphic specialist for The Salvation Army Golden State Divisional Headquarters, for the design of this book's cover.

Thanks to Maisie Fong, my dedicated assistant, for her hard work in supporting me. She is always available, and I'm grateful.

I owe a special debt of thanks to so many pastors, apostles, and evangelists who have inspired me and helped me to grow in my understanding of scripture and of God's love as listed in the Resource section of this book their sermons, YouTube messages, and books help build my faith in God.

You can find some of their sermons on my website http://victoryglory.com/

To all of these and many more, I thank you for helping me to bring the story to the page showing that God is good.

# About the Author

Margaret Liu Collins is called to share the Good News about God in every aspect of her life from her intimate life with her family to her business practices and philanthropy, and into her leadership and testimony in her Christian community and beyond.

She was born in Chongqing, China, and attended high school, St. Stephen's Girls College, Hong Kong. She later graduated with a Bachelor of Science degree from the University of California, Berkeley. After being a science teacher, she later became the founder and CEO of a real estate brokerage firm, Liu Realty, Inc., and is the founder and CEO of Liu International Management LLC.

Margaret has served as a director of nonprofit organizations including Grace Cathedral, The Episcopal

Dioceses of Northern California, California Pacific Medical Center, The University of California Berkeley Foundation Board, and the San Francisco Symphony. Her for-profit board memberships include Cmos, ComplianceEase, and Servgate.

With God's prompting, Margaret has supported her Alma mater, the University of California, Berkeley, establishing a fellowship endowment, "T. O. Liu Memorial Fellowship" in Helen Willis Neuroscience Institute in honor of her father. In 2010, she established an undergraduate scholarship to provide financial resources for deserving students who come from families led by single parents.

San Francisco Business Times, in 2011, named Margaret one of the "150 Most Influential Women in Bay Area Business".

In 2016, Margaret endowed Chair Professorship in Traumatic Brain Injury to world-renowned neurosurgeon Geoffrey T. Manley, MD, Ph.D., Professor and Vice Chairman Department of Neurological Surgery, UCSF Weill Institute of Neurosciences and Chief of Neurological Surgery, Zuckerberg San Francisco General Hospital, and Trauma Center.

In 2013, she collaborated with her late Aunt, Qin Ziao-men, to write a book about her beloved father *A Twentieth-Century Chinese Profile Tien Oung Liu* available on Amazon.

Margaret and her adoring husband, Ted Collins, split their time between homes in San Francisco and Sonoma County, taking special pleasure in watching their grandchildren grow.

Margaret offers support for fellow Christians along with inspiring articles, videos, and resources on her website at: VictoryGlory.com

Printed in the USA
CPSIA information can be obtained
at www.ICGtesting.com
JSHW011512130823
46416JS00007B/100